THE READING MIRACLE
The Universal Reading Method Discovered

...as told by

Craig Collins

Printed in the United States of America

First Printing, 2019

ISBN: 978-0-578-61707-7

www.universalreadingmethod.com

AUTHOR

Craig Collins, CEO and Cofounder, Universal Reading Method

Table of Contents

PROLOGUE

As the car pulled up in my driveway, I witnessed Zane, a 13-year-old boy, crying, with his hooded sweatshirt pulled up over his head and the bill of his baseball cap pulled over his face, sitting in the backseat of his mom's car.

When I bent down next to the car door to listen to him, I could feel the heat from his body and smell the fragrance of sincere tears. He was overcome with fear and today was not a day he wanted to be a failure…one more time…and he told me so.

I assured him I understood and that it was not necessary for him to learn to read today. It is not my practice to force someone to learn to read.

After another private, brief conversation with his mom, Zane climbed out of the car and walked into my house and sat down on the couch near the fireplace, still with his hood over his face and crying softly.

As he peered at me from his corner lookout on the red couch in the living room—his mother had just walked out the door—he was drying his eyes and sat waiting for my next words.

I sat next to him, speaking softly, and said, "I need your help. I have never been trained as a teacher, so I do not know how to help a young person your age overcome your fear of something you have learned to feel is real, like a teacher would. In addition, I have never been a father of my own sons, so I can't help you that way either. So, the only thing I can be to you is a friend and in being that friend I want you to know that I have walked the road you are on right now and have been around the corner where you believe the Boogie Man is gonna get you . . . and that this time, I want to assure you, the Boogie Man is not there."

After Zane pulled off his hooded sweatshirt and removed his ball cap in preparation for the next 2 1/2 hours, I reached my hand out to shake his. As I shook his hand and he looked into my eyes for the first time, he leaned forward and whispered to me, "I really can't read! There may be something wrong with me."

As we sat down at the table to view the Universal Reading Method online, he watched me closely with apprehension. I felt he still believed he was going to fail, one more time.

When I told him, "My brother Doug, the developer of this reading method I am going to share with you, was unable to read for 30 years, and that he was only 8 years old—" Zane took a breath and began to relax, and some of the color returned to his face. For this young man had been told a story many times about himself—most of it very embarrassing, none of it true—all of it bad.

Had he been born stupid and dumb? Was this going to be the final proving of his broken and disabled brain? Was his fate to be sealed today or was there to be an opening?

I am going to continue this story from the viewpoint of my student:

As I viewed Craig on the computer screen teaching me his Universal Reading Method . . . *first concept, second concept, third concept . . . FASTER, LOUDER . . .* I began to get it. I placed my feet firmly on the ground. *Fourth concept . . .* feel my lips upturned and smiling, my breath is easing . . . long and short . . . I get it . . . *Fifth concept . . .*

sounds, all of the sounds, where to pause and see the syllables.

Sitting up straight, leaning forward, I am feeling something in my brain . . . a tingly sensation . . . *Sixth concept* . . . I just read a really long word. I did not run out of the room. The word I read is longer than any word I have ever seen. No need to hide . . . just looked at the 9 syllables . . . and not really thinking too much . . . *One long, two short . . . pause* . . . hearing the sounds. I read a 29-letter word! It was actually easy. Why didn't someone tell me this before? Wow . . . just read the long word with the 9 syllables. No words are that long that I have ever read before. Wow . . . I got it!

My fate has not been sealed . . . it has been opened . . . opened to unknown places I have never traveled. I am really curious; will I be able to read other words too?

During my walk . . . alone . . . no, with self, Craig told me . . . not alone . . . I am powerful. I am going to return, and I am going to remember all of this. I just read this really long word . . . and all of the letters came together and made sounds. I feel the wind in my hair . . . no matter that it is cold . . . I am warm inside . . . I am free . . . for the first time in a long while . . . I feel free...no more tears!

I am sitting back at the table. My head is kind of spinning . . . LOL . . . feels good. Now, time to review what I have learned. I am putting the information in my brain . . . my way . . . my way . . . no one else is telling me how to think. Craig said, "Your brain and your way are the best!" I have never heard that before . . . but it feels good! The sounds on the review sheet come easy to me . . . like I have known them all my life . . . but they just didn't make sense . . . before.

Oh my, the exceptional sounds are easy . . . like a master

gamesman I take them all in: ck, black; ed, walked and played; ie, believe . . . and now I am at the end . . . and all 42 of the exceptions are planted on my brain and I easily read the words connected to them.

There is nothing more for me to learn. The computer screen goes dark. Is that all there is to learn to read?

I am standing, I am reaching forward, I am smiling big, and I am ready to challenge anything . . . Bring those words on . . . Let's do it!

Wow, I just read 475 very big words. College words. Words I had never seen or recognized in print before. I never would have attempted to read them before . . . not even one of them . . . I just didn't believe I could. They didn't make sense . . . NOW they do!

As my mom returns to pick me up and walks through the front door, she immediately asks, "How did it go?"

I stand up proudly and announce, "I am Brilliant!" and then I read all of the 475 College Level words to her, faster than I did with Craig.

"I am Brilliant!"

The day after our instruction, Zane's mother Kady received this email note:

Hi Kady,

I was going to email you after school today and let you know how impressed I was with Zane in class. He was like I've never seen him before—focused, taking beautiful notes, and asking questions that were impressive. It'll be interesting to see his progress this upcoming semester, but he is definitely off to a great 2017 in my class so far.

Zane's Teacher, 7th Grade Science

Vista Magnet Middle School, Vista, California

VIDEO INTERVIEW OF ZANE:

https://www.youtube.com/watch?v=tc_sNIbzGwg

It's transformations such as Zane's that fuel my passion, as well as other people's, to spread the Universal Reading Method to as many challenged readers as possible.

AUTHOR'S NOTE

"If they cannot learn the way we teach. . . then we need to teach them the way they learn!"

During my life, I have enjoyed some quite exciting times as an Investigative Consultant, solving mysteries, often in other countries. There were many challenges and even at times my life was at risk. While working on a case there are big "aha" moments when I realized I was on the right track and it will only be a short time until the mystery is solved. I called these times "pulling-the-bunny-out-of-the-hat."

From the first time I watched someone transform into a reader in only 2 ½ hours I suspected there was something more happening in the brains of our students than learning to read. Discovering what was happening has become the greatest mystery that I will ever solve. My brother, Doug Collins, the person who discovered our reading method, has definitely "pulled-the-bunny-out-of-the-hat" for the students who have benefited from our Universal Reading Method.

Please join me as my investigation takes me to many parts of the world and eventually deep within the brains of my students provided by brain imaging. Clearly, the students transformed me and opened up my mind as our instruction transformed them, in more ways than reading.

* * *

As the train pulled out of Chicago on my way to Toronto, several years later, I reflected on my "life changing" event that took place in a hospital in 2006.

Sitting up in a hospital bed, after surgery for a kidney infection, I distinctly remembered sitting in a chair across the room, looking at the surgical table I had been placed on earlier, peering beyond the surgical gowns of two doctors and several nurses and realizing I was Me, watching ME on the table. Everyone was scrambling around frantically, evidently my heart had stopped for a short while. Once the anesthesiologist got involved, I believe they used the paddles. The next thing I knew, I was waking up from the anesthesia and being carted by two young orderlies back to my hospital room, where a dear friend awaited me.

What I remember about this near-death experience was when I was finally situated in my room, I felt like a major transformation had occurred. I felt like I had an urgent mission I had been instructed to achieve. My desire was profound and the message to me was with great volume and energy. At that instance, I turned the corner from being an investigator and consultant and was on my way to another chapter in my life. I just didn't know how it was going to unfold.

It was during that time I began to realize all of the psychological, analytical and intuitive training and life experiences I had acquired over the years was to be used to offer to the world a significant transformational gift. I could feel my life-work ahead was going to be monumental, requiring my life to change in many ways.

It was when I spoke to my brother Doug, and he told me he had discovered seven, never-before-seen, concepts to learning to read English, that I began to come to terms with how I was going to spend this part of my life and how his life-changing contribution was going to impact the world because of my participation.

It was monumental when I realized that he really had 'broken-the- code' to reading. I said to myself, with excitement, "Our world needs to know about Doug's discovery, and he is too shy to do it by himself!" That was when I knew that one of the reasons I was alive right now and here on earth was to TEACH THE WORLD TO READ ENGLISH. Little did I know that this decision would send me off to embark on the greatest adventure of my life and take me all over the world.

I was on my way to discovering the evidence we needed to prove the instruction that had been revealed to my brother would transform the majority of learners with reading challenges in the world.

As I began to travel the United States, Canada, the UK and Hawaii on our World Wise Universal Reading Method Literacy Tour, my travels introduced me to many cultures and a diverse population of students who were reading challenged with every type of diagnosis that you can imagine. Many professionals were trying to diagnose them, but few were listening to them and teaching them to read. I was listening intensely, and I was watching them transform.

I became more passionate and excited each day, as I taught and watched hundreds of successful reading transformations take place. I knew when I started that I needed to build a case in favor of our reading method much like I would a legal case. It was my investigator-self that immediately began collecting the "evidence-based" proof we needed to establish our credibility as the only reading method that truly transformed learners from challenged readers of

English, no matter where in the world they lived or what their reason for not being able to read was, into confident, competent readers, **in only 2 ½ hours**.

If you are experiencing any skepticism that it will work for someone you know and love, I completely understand. Imagine what it was for me to step into new communities and countries and teach challenged readers I didn't know. It was your and my skepticism that motivated me forward. The folks I met were all different and couldn't read for different reasons. For you, I have proven that our Universal Reading Method is the "Real Thing," the absolute answer to learning to read English.

Looking back on my travels, I am humored by all the challenges I had to overcome. Many times, I did so without any money in the bank. Sometimes, I did not have food to eat. Twice my backpack was stolen with all my credit cards, passport and personal identification lost. And then magically, or I should say, spiritually, things would just fall back together. It became obvious, I was always "falling-together," never apart, as I felt many times.

On Maui, after my backpack was stolen, I found St. Theresa's Catholic Meals for the Homeless and taught homeless folks to read for free. It seemed like each time I taught folks for free then the universe rewarded me and invited me to the next level.

What if you couldn't read, no matter what age you are, you just can't figure out what those letters do, how they make sounds, and for the life of you, how they make words? It is all just a big blur for you, and yet many of your friends sitting right next to you in class, even some of the ones who don't seem very smart, can read! You may come to believe there is something "wrong" with your brain.

After a while, when you are still too young to be evaluated, your teacher is describing you as some broken child to your mom, your friends are laughing at you when you attempt to read in the reading circle, and now you are feeling really 'dumb and stupid'.

Pretty soon, you are being placed discreetly in one of those "special classes" for people like you, and when you walk into the room where your mom is talking to your teacher, they both get quiet. Your mom looks worried and sad and the teacher looks relieved she has made her point. It feels like there is a cloud of shame around you. Even your school chums are unkind to you.

Ok…so while this was all happening, as teachers began referring their challenged students to me, sometimes, as a kind of last-ditch effort, I began to observe and consider something more profound than I had ever considered before: Possibly, someone who cannot read is actually very intelligent, even brilliant. They just can't read!

Knowing how to read was proving not to be a measurement for intelligence. My learners' personalities appeared to change when they become readers. Just like Zane had announced, "I am Brilliant, Mom," immediately after he read fluently 475 post-high-school words when before he was unable to read 4th grade words.

As I continued my travels, I met folks, young and old, who could barely read small three- and four-letter words. I was honored to witness, breath-by-breath, their transformation from extreme frustration, many with tears of shame, while reading small words to reading long multi-syllable words, college-level words. I truly was amazed listening to them reading from books without pictures and with smaller type fonts. They were delighted and proud to share with me the story, after reading aloud to me. Many reported that when they read it was like someone outside of them was reading them a story and it was easy for them to remember what they read.

Something miraculous was happening to each and every one of my students. I wanted to tell everyone and early on I was honored to be invited to be a speaker at TEDx La Jolla, in California. If you would like to watch the TEDx La Jolla-Craig Collins-The Universal Reading Method video please go to:

https://www.youtube.com/watch?v=zAPa_e3EGx0

Are you beginning to understand why I am so excited? I want you to share my passion! I want you to join me in my quest to bring Light to a world that is filled with darkness for millions of children and adults in the US and in different parts of the world.

That is what this book is about!

It is about the students in San Diego who transformed into competent and confident readers who motivated me to take off across the United States in search of the evidence, and to begin sharing our transformation with learners everywhere.

It is about my students in Canada and those in Scotland, England and Ireland. And those I found as I traveled who were from Germany, France, China, Japan and Ghana. Young people, very old people, men and women who have never read a full page of writing without feeling panicked and challenged.

Our students had been labeled "developmentally disabled" (whatever that means), dyslexic, autistic, and some just believed they were born with a "dumb and stupid" brain.

One woman was in a convalescent home and was diagnosed with Alzheimer's syndrome; several had had multiple strokes and a heart attack and one man was paralyzed on one-half of his body and, when we began our instruction, slurred his speech . After 2 ½ hours of instruction, all of them were reading again, better than they had before their injury. Many were from, English speaking and foreign countries with a whole host of accents and different ways of saying things.

Since you are reading this book, you may have a special reason for our coming to your attention that has something to do with someone you know who has difficulty with reading. Possibly, you are a frustrated child educator, a parent, a husband or wife, a friend, a school principal, a therapist or someone who had your own challenges and struggles with reading and wish reading English was easier for you?

You may sense it inside of you and have watched someone close to you, possibly your child, lose that special excitement about learning because they just couldn't grasp that 'reading thing' at school. You may have remained silent, not saying anything, taking responsibility for birthing a child who, the teachers are telling you, may be a "little slow" or "behind the others in the class." You may have a student who has been told and/or believes he is "dumb or stupid" because of his or her reading challenges. We are excited to meet you and immediately take this weight off your shoulders.

I began to realize that the time has come when I can no longer sit quietly by and watch the increasing numbers of young men and women sitting confused, bored, and without hope, because the reading method that is being provided leaves them confused and, in a fog, feeling 'less-than'.

I want to invite you to join me and take action. We can no longer turn a blind eye and forget that the child we once knew, when he/she first started out in school, was excited to learn. We cannot turn a blind eye to the fact something happened to make them lose their spark, their excitement about learning. What we know about education is that it must be ever-changing with a goal to meet the needs of the students. We have taken that action! We are teaching them to read.

As you travel with me on our literacy tour and as you read about the transformation of our students, we are inviting you to join us and to realize we have experienced a remarkable educational unfolding that is personal and inspiring, an unfolding that has never been seen before. It is our vision that many of our students will become the brilliant leaders we will need in the future.

Each chapter is offered with a willingness to look at reading and the brain in a new way, using neuroscience and with a new understanding of how it receives information via plasticity. We offer this story to you with excitement as we search for scientific results from our MEG brain imaging research at the University of California, San Diego (UCSD).

As we move forward, we do so because of the courage and tenacity of our students and a firm belief we have stumbled onto something that is just this short of a miracle.

As this book touches, as it crystallizes something that has been festering within you for a long time, as it awakens a new hope for those you know who are challenged with reading English, then we will have gone a long way in changing our world in a very positive way. Shout it to the world with us. Together we can bring about this change.

Now on with our story and our adventure…one that we see no end to.

Craig Collins, CEO

Universal Reading Method, Corp

Chapter 1

Doug and Craig Collins, The Men Behind the Magic (Not How the Universal Reading Method Came To Be)

Doug Collins, my brother, was an emotionally tortured man who was challenged with reading words ever since he was very young. During his growing up years he attempted to learn as much as possible about the processes and methods of learning to read, and yet he still struggled.

Doug was able to complete college because his instructors accommodated his reading disability by providing oral exams. After college, he applied and was accepted into law school, but oral exams were something the law school did not provide. When he confided in a professor that he was too hindered by his reading challenges to be able to attend law school, the professor told him, "You don't have to memorize every little detail. You can learn by understanding concepts. Large bodies of information can be simplified and learned by placing them together in easy to learn concepts."

It was soon after this, the next morning, that Doug received a flash of insight, an epiphany that revealed to him the seven concepts for reading English.

After receiving this knowledge, he was able to attend law school, excel in his classes, and learn and understand all the required reading. Upon completing his studies, I am proud to say, Doug graduated at the top of his class. But how could this be?

Many years later, during the winter of 2007, a year after my life-changing near-death experience, my brother introduced me to his reading method. He called it The Collins Reading Method and was now, successfully teaching students to read at his private pre-school in the San Fernando Valley, to students supervised by the Regional Center in San Diego, and to students at a nearby high school who wanted to take the SAT test and hoped to attend college. Basically, his students were folks who could not read above a 4th grade level.

After an excited parent watched his child read for the first time, the parent called the local television station news program and told them about his son's transformation. Doug was interviewed by Jim Wilkerson, a news reporter in San Diego, and demand for his reading method began to grow. Later that year, Doug successfully taught several more students who were labeled as the students least likely to succeed and enter college to take the SAT.   All of them attended college the next semester.

I was skeptical about Doug's discovery but knew my brother always told the truth, even when we were youngsters growing up in Palos Verdes.

What I did not know was how and why his reading method worked. Why were students as young as 3 ½ grasping what I, and most people, believed to be something very difficult to learn, and never in just 2 ½ hours?

How could all this be possible? I had to research the word epiphany to find out.

An example of an epiphany is how the Periodic Table that hung on the wall in your chemistry class came to be. In 1869, Dmitri Mendeleev, a Russian scientist, had a dream and then sat down and wrote out the whole chart, inclusive of the properties of eight elements yet to be discovered.

According to Wikipedia, "The word epiphany was used to describe a scientific breakthrough, a religious or philosophical discovery…an enlightening realization that allows a problem or situation to be understood from a new and deeper perspective.

"Epiphanies generally follow a process of significant thought about a problem…. Often, they are triggered by a new and key piece of information, but importantly, a depth of prior knowledge is required to allow the leap of understanding."

Even though I was sure this is how my brother was gifted these reading tools, I still needed to be convinced that they worked consistently.

TEACHING ESL STUDENTS AT A COMMUNITY COLLEGE

I needed to observe Doug's method being taught, and I needed to bring him students he had never met. It was kind of like the discovery you do when you are watching a magician do magic tricks on a stage. So, I brought Doug people I knew who could not read English: adults, children of different ages, folks who were from foreign countries, students he never met before.

Each time I brought Doug a student to teach, I would sit quietly and watch. Some of the students came alone and some brought their parents. But no matter whoever I introduced him to, whoever sat with him for the 2 1/2 hours repeating his seven concepts, when they arrived they could not read, and when they left it was very obvious that a significant change in their reading ability and their personality had taken place. Not only could they all read now, they seemed more confident, more outgoing, more verbal, and some were even a tad cocky.

One thought I had was that Doug must be a very good teacher and it was his charisma that was transforming the people I was bringing to him. But the answer was not about Doug's personality or mine, it was about his reading method.

I had observed him teach students, one-on-one, so my next question was: Could he teach more than one student at a time? What about a class of students and what if the students could not speak English and were from Mexico and China?

With that question in mind, I met an English as a Second Language (ESL) instructor at Palomar College in San Diego County. After several conversations and hearing from her how she was teaching a class of students, all of whom were either from Mexico or China, and whose parents did not speak English at home, she decided to let Doug teach her evening ESL class. It was nearing the end of the semester and her students had not become readers with the instruction she had been providing them.

Doug's plan was to teach them, all at the same time, in a classroom The Collins Reading Method (later to be renamed the Universal Reading Method). It was important to us that we pre-tested each student a week prior to the instruction to establish their reading ability and for them to have a benchmark of their own.

Using the Wide Range Achievement Test 3 (WRAT 3) Pre-test developed by Harcourt Brace, it was determined that most of the students were reading at a 4th grade reading level. Many, when we pre-tested them, did not speak to us in English. One person, a young Mexican mother, I actually begged that she return and learn to read with us.

The next day after all the students had been pre-tested, Doug stood in front of the room, with his reading method written on the chalkboard, and taught The Collins Reading Method to the whole class. I was amazed to listen to each of the students voluntarily repeating each of his concepts in unison with others in the class. It actually seemed to go more smoothly when the students were working off of each other, in a group.

It was the most amazing class I had ever observed. It was obvious as he went from concept one to concept six during the first hour of instruction that each student was completely focused on learning them. Even the students who were unable to read any of the words on the pre-test were energetically and successfully following along with the other students. There were no behavior issues to deal with.

After just one hour of instruction, I observed each of the students in the class had become more outgoing and some were chatting with each other in English, in contrast to speaking only Spanish or Chinese when they arrived, as they walked outside to take their required fifteen-minute consolidation 'brain break'.

At the end of the instruction, Doug had the students break up into two teams and play a word game using a long list of multi-syllable words from the General Education Diploma (GED). I enjoyed hearing them laughing and having a good time. At the end of the game each student had successfully read multi-syllable words that were college-level words and at a significant higher degree of difficulty than they had been tested with in the pre-test.

Two days later, after our instruction, as the students came back to class with renewed enthusiasm and excitement, we began administering the standardized WRAT 3 Post-test. Doug, our team of testers, and I were amazed by the results.

One of the women, a single mother of two children, had been unable to read even one word on the pre-test and only spoke in Spanish to us on the first day. I had to beg her to come back the next day to participate in our instruction. When she showed up, I watched her from the back of the class and could hear her grasp each concept. During the chalk board game, she was one of the best readers on her team. The energy in the room was ecstatic.

The evidence we collected teaching this ESL class informed us that if we could create an online reading method then we could teach whole classes with it and all students, no matter how large the class, would read with fluency, college-level words with understandable pronunciation. I imagined filling a large theater with students and transforming hundreds of challenged readers at one time.

Students from foreign countries often do not speak English openly because they fear they will be laughed at because of their pronunciation. When I heard these students speaking English in front of me, I realized that their speech pathology had shifted as well, with their self-confidence allowing them to speak English in a manner they had never attempted before.

After many more students transformed, I became motivated to

accept an invitation to teach several students in Minnesota, one who was reported to have been diagnosed with Asperger Syndrome, reported by his mother, having receiving an early childhood vaccine and then I went on to Chicago to teach students at the local library.

With each impressive transformation, I became more and more motivated to continue to travel to different parts of the world, in search of more challenged readers, more evidence to share with you. It became logical that if I was going to teach "the world to read" I had best travel the world.

As the word spread via social media, I began to get invited to different cities by families to teach their children and the children of their friends, and often the parents themselves. Our travels took us across the mid-western United States, up into Canada, to New York, across the pond to the United Kingdom, back down the West Coast of Northern California and over to Hawaii.

With each successful transformation, it became obvious to me if our students had not been introduced to our Universal Reading Method, they most likely would have never learned to read. Most of them had given up and just believed that reading was not something they would ever be able to do. Several of my adult students confessed to me that they were so convinced there was something wrong with their brain that they did not marry because of their fear they would pass their "broken brain" onto their children.

We invite you to meet, with more intimate details, some of our formerly reading-challenged students and share in their story and transformation.

Chapter 2

Dyslexia, an Amazing Personal Journey With Ellen

I had been teaching the Universal Reading Method for only a short time and was telling my friend Ellen, who I had known for several years, how totally amazed and impressed I was with the changes I observed with people who experienced our method. At the time, I was the sole teacher, with my brother, and had not created our video instruction yet.

After sharing with her that I had, to my surprise, taught a person who was a scientist who could not read, and in just a little over 2 hours he had read fluently for the first time, Ellen leaned towards me and whispered, "Craig, I have never told you, but I can't read!

"All through grade school, junior high, and high school I was always challenged with reading!" Ellen confided. "When it came for most of my friends to leave home and go to college, I was not with them. There are men I did not date nor marry because I was embarrassed about my lack of reading skills!

"Today, I am in my late 50s and when I am invited to a party, I have to write down the directions on a scrap of paper and follow the instructions, one step at a time. As I come to each street, I have to get out of my car and compare what I have written on the scrap of paper with the name of the street on the street sign. Yes, I have to stop at each sign, and if it is the wrong street, I have to drive to the next one and get out again! I leave extra early, but with the effort it takes me, I am rarely on time anywhere!

With her moist eyes focused on mine, Ellen exclaimed, "Craig, I want you to teach me your reading method! What do I have to lose?"

We immediately set a date and time for the next day and we both showed up to the dining room table in her apartment. Ellen was a focused learner and easily succeeded learning each of our seven concepts. I think she was surprised, at the end, when she read hundreds of words that before she never would have even attempted or looked at.

It was after 2 hours and 15 minutes of instruction and reading all of the words, over 300 words, that Ellen announced with urgency, "Thank you for teaching me, now I need you to leave. There is something I need to do! I will call you later!" I remember it was still light and around 6:30 pm in the early evening.

Not quite understanding, but definitely wishing not to crowd her or interfere with her plans, I went to the door and left her sitting at the table still looking at the list of words she had just read. As I walked out the door, I looked over my shoulder and saw a big smile on her face.

About five hours later, around midnight, I received a phone call from Ellen. Her first words were: "I did it! I finished all of them! And, I understood all of them!"

Of course, I asked, "What? What did you do?"

"I just read 52 weeks, a whole year's worth, of James Rone Newsletters!" James Rone is a motivational speaker who publishes a newsletter that Ellen had received every week for a year. When they arrived, she had placed them in a folder, always telling herself she was going to "get around to" looking at them and try to read them.

Now, she had sat down on the floor in her office with the overflowing notebook and had read all of them, from cover to cover. This was one very proud woman! It was as if she had cut the fire out of a dragon that had been following her around all of her life.

I am still friends with Ellen, and she is still reading. Once again, it was amazing to have participated in, what always appears to me to be, a miracle of reading transformation.

Possibly you are beginning to wonder how we transform our Learners into readers and would like meet some of them, including Ellen? Please go to this site on your computer, phone or iPad: **www.youtube.com/watch?time_continue=27&v=xpZZ9-DALxA**

Chapter 3

The Most Improved Student Award

*"The more that you read, the more things that you will know.
The more you learn the more places you will go."*

Dr. Seuss

While driving up to Manhattan Beach from San Diego to teach Beau, an 8-year-old boy, our Universal Reading Method, I thought about my brother Doug and our growing up in Palos Verdes Estates and my many adventures at the beaches from Lunada Bay all the way to Santa Barbara.

Doug, the creator of the Universal Reading Method, once lived and attended college at nearby El Camino Community College and I remembered visiting him and hanging out at the beach.

As I crossed over Pacific Coast Highway, I began to feel my anticipation for teaching today's student. We had not developed our video yet, and thus, I taught him myself, first pre-testing him to determine his reading ability, then I shared our seven concepts on two large printed sheets of plastic-covered paper, a long list of multi-syllable words, and then had him read from one of his favorite books.

At school it wasn't until Beau was introduced to math problems with words in them that it became important to him to learn to read. Prior to the word problems he was awarded for his ability in math. Beau is a very bright and determined young man and did not like that he was challenged with reading.

So, enter Craig and the Universal Reading Method . . . and within just 2 ½ hours, this young man was easily reading from a vocabulary list and from a book he had been asked to read by his teacher at school.

Several weeks later, his mom called and shared with me, "Beau just received an award at his school for the Most Improved Student in his class." I could hear and feel her smile over the phone.

Often it is during math class that teachers become aware that some of their students have difficulty solving their math word problems because they cannot read.

Chapter 4

A First Grader Reads at a Fifth Grade Level

"I have got the key to the castle in the air, but whether I can unlock the door remains to be seen."

Louisa May Alcott

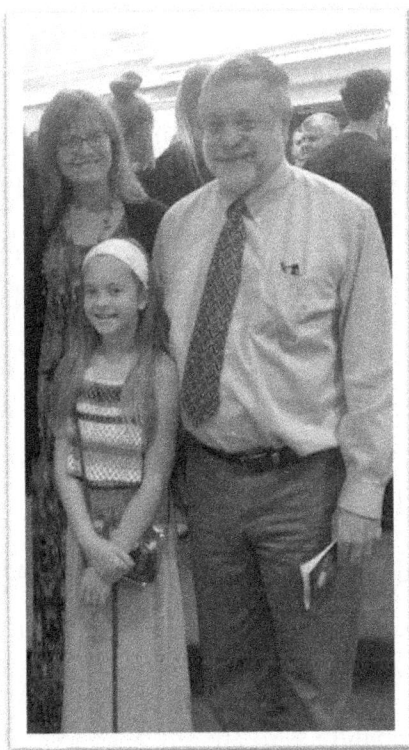

The Hubachers

After teaching Beau to read in Manhattan Beach, I felt like celebrating, so I made a phone call to some old friends of mine who lived nearby, John and Anna-Pia Hubacher, and they said, "Come on by, we would love to see you."

While sitting in their kitchen talking with Anna-Pia, I began to tell her about my life and teaching folks to read. When I mentioned that Doug has taught preschool age children, Anna-Pia suggested that I teach their 5-year-old daughter Alexandria our Universal Reading Method.

So, after a quick roundtrip run to my car, I pulled out my magic sheets with the Universal Reading Method and asked their little girl, "Would you like to learn to read?"

Looking at me with inquisitive eyes, Alexandria shrugged her shoulders a little and said, "OK," with a little hesitance. Now, remember she is only 5 years old and was really having a fun time playing with her dolls, so I was a surprise interruption.

Right from the start, it was obvious to me that Alexandria was understanding and repeating confidently everything that I was teaching her. So, after a little less than an hour, I sent her off for her 15-minute break. Mom gave her some juice and then she ran outside to play in the backyard.

While outside, speaking in a low voice to Anna-Pia, "Although my brother has many times, I, personally, have never taught someone this young before. Your daughter is responding to the instructions like the children I have taught who are older. I want to be very careful not to tire her out so she will finish all of the instruction. She is getting it."

After about 15 minutes Alexandria returned from playing outside and then I had her spend another 15 minutes looking at the papers by herself and reviewing what I had been teaching, without my assistance or involvement. Regardless of her young age, she very methodically looked at the review sheets and I heard her going over all of the sounds by herself, out-loud.

After she completed her 15-minute "self-study," I continued by telling her what the exceptional sounds are like that do not follow the concepts she has just learned, and I listened to her accurately repeat them: ous, jealous; ious, serious; ing, sing; ong, song . . .and so on.

After she confidently repeated all the exceptional sounds for me, I asked her if she would like to read some long words and try out what she has learned about reading.

As she began to stand, she very confidently and politely looked me straight in the eyes and said, "No, I am ready to go outside and play now! Thank you!"

It was so cute.

So, I said, "Absolutely!" as I watched her run outside, after first grabbing an oatmeal cookie from a plate sitting on the table.

I looked at Anna-Pia and she looked at me and we both shrugged our shoulders, smiled and agreed, "No reason to make her do anything more. She does not have to prove to us that she can use the information she took in.'

Once a child knows how to read it is important to keep track of the books in your home you do not want them to read because of their possible adult content.

So, 18 months later, out of the blue, John contacted me, excited after talking to Alexandria's first grade teacher, and told me this amazing story about his daughter's reading. I asked him to send me an email about their exchange. I love this letter from John.

Dear Craig,

As you know, our daughter Alexandria is now in the middle of the school year of the first grade in elementary school.

We just received her report card and it stated she is reading at a 5th grade level. The teacher feels she is pretty much teaching herself to read, as she is a voracious reader in the morning and at night at home.

Her spelling is also very high accuracy, with difficult words. And, she is only in the middle of the First Grade and six years old.

Remember, eighteen months ago, when she was 5 years old, while visiting, you taught her the Universal Reading Method. It appears you have given her the "keys to the kingdom" for reading. She appears to have learned, from you something very essential and fundamental that has caused her to excel to this extraordinary level of accomplishment. And she thinks this is all totally normal and is just progressing at her own warp speed, without any requests or pressure from us.

It was reported to me by her teacher, she is farther ahead in reading than all of the other children in her class, and most of the students in her school, including the fifth graders. Significant to us, she is the only one to have received your seven reading concepts.

Although we always suspected she was bright before you taught her, she is definitely expressing it now. It is amazing to think of the power and advantage in life she has acquired, by accessing and acquiring such advanced reading skills at such an early age.

It brings me great joy to see my daughter's intellect, sense of finding out about the world, level of curiosity, confidence, and deep interaction with books, ideas, and stories, profoundly expanded because of your involvement with her.

Think of the possibilities if the whole country or world learned to read at such a level at an early age. Our amazement as parents is almost beyond measure, and our gratitude is the highest possible.

With deep thanks for your gift to our family,

John Hubacher

Pantheon Research Inc.

In August of 2015 I checked in with John Hubacher again. It had been four years since I had taught Alexandria. She was ten years old and entering the 4th grade. John told me she is the top student in her class and possibly the whole school. (Her school includes 5th Grade.)

She reads at a high school level and scores in the top 1% of all students her age in the nation. She has received the highest marks in all her subjects for the last three years. Most of her schooling has been independent study.

She enjoys adult subjects more than 4th grade subjects and they are looking at the possibility of her attending a school for high ability and gifted students because it is apparent, she would benefit by being with students who excel in school like she does.

Chapter 5

One Of The Richest Men In London

"When I was at school, if you couldn't read, they called you thick. I hated reading as a kid and as an adult I've organized my life to avoid it as much as possible." Andreas Panayiotou, from an article in the *London Evening Standard*.

While researching the illiteracy statistics in England, I came across an article in the *London Evening Standard,* "Secrets of the £400 Million Tycoon Who Does Not Know How to Read." It was an article about a man named Andreas Panayiotou, of Greek descent, who was announcing his lifelong struggle with reading English.

Mr. Panayiotou is the man responsible for the creation and development of the Waldorf/Hilton Hotels in England and many parts of the world.

"I am doing it because the Evening Standard's *expose' has moved and shocked me. I am amazed to see the problem in our schools is still so bad. I'd hate any kid to go through what I have."* He talked to the reporter about his "darkest secret" to help expose the scandal of illiteracy in London.

Mr. Panayiotou was courageous as he spoke to the reporter about his own fitful time and embarrassment with learning to read in school. Despite this handicap, he was able to overcome it by delegating and surrounding himself with others who would read to him. In doing this he became tremendously successful.

I invite you to read the article, published in the *London Evening Standard*, that inspired me to seek out and teach this great man to read.

London ● Evening Standard
standard.co.uk

Secret of the £400 million tycoon who does not know how to read

 David Cohen 3 Jun 2011

Ph: Rebecca Reid

I am sitting in the sumptuous West End office of businessman *Andreas Panayiotou* as he scans the front page of the *Evening*

Standard and attempts to read it out loud. He begins normally, but by the second sentence he has become hesitant, using his forefinger to guide him. He delivers each word slowly and deliberately. In the third paragraph, he comes to a halt.

"What's that word?" he asks, pointing to 'receipts'. In the next sentence he is stymied again, this time by 'exposé'. Mr. Panayiotou is a 45 year old in his prime with every reason to be super-confident, but now his hands start writhing and he begins to sweat in his £3,000 Tom Ford suit.

The self-made British mogul, conservatively said to be worth £400million and ranked 200th on the Rich List, is about to describe his "secret shame" for the first time - he has never learned to read.

"When I was at school, if you couldn't read, they called you *thick*. I hated reading as a kid and as an adult I've organised my life to avoid it as much as possible. *My PA reads my emails to me over the phone while I drive into work and I dictate replies. My lawyers handle legal documents, and my accountants deal with the financial stuff.*"

The mere act of trying to read transports him back to the shame he felt as a child. "You know what?" he said, taking hold of the newspaper again. "I might be sitting here in this office, but right now, in my mind, I am back there, seven years old, in my old class at Wellington Way primary school in Bow.

"I can remember it with absolute clarity. The teacher is going round the room asking different kids to read. I am praying he won't call me. He calls one kid. Then another. I am getting hot and anxious. Sod's law, third kid, he turns to me. 'I don't wanna!' I say. 'Why?' he asks. I don't want to say in front of everyone that I can't read. The teacher starts shouting. He thinks I'm being cheeky. He throws me out.

"That was the last time I was ever asked to read. After that the teacher would skip me to avoid a confrontation. I learned to memorise whole words, what they look like, but I never did learn to read in the conventional sense, and I left school at 14 without a single GCSE.

That moment has stayed with me because it was the day I realised I had a problem. Everything - my massive drive to prove myself as a 'somebody', my rigid discipline, my pride in what I've achieved -

stems from the feelings of shame and inadequacy I experienced of being 'perpetually behind' all the other kids and unable to read."

The *Standard* has published shocking new figures exposing illiteracy in London. One in three children has no books of their own at home; one in three 11year olds in parts of the capital still has a reading age of as low as seven. Poet Benjamin Zephaniah has talked of how dyslexic people tend to go "one of two ways": conquering their fears and flourishing, or ending up in jail. Mr. Panayiotou, one of the million adult Londoners who the National Literacy Trust say are functionally illiterate, exemplifies the former.

The London-born son of Greek Cypriots, his achievements are extraordinary. He owns a £40million Gulfstream G450 jet, a £12million Mangusta 130 yacht, and two Cessna Citation jets. He lives on a 20-acre plot in Epping Forest with second wife Susan and their three daughters aged seven, 12 and 14 (he also has two older sons from his first marriage). He has stables, a helipad, gym, tennis court and five lakes.

This morning he came to work in his Range Rover, but could equally have driven his Ferrari Enzo, Lamborghini LP700, Rolls-Royce Phantom convertible, or £1.2million Bugatti Veyron. His Italian marble-floored office is the size of a tennis court. Pictures and models of his planes and yacht decorate his office. "As a child, I tried my best to read, but the words would get scrambled up in my brain and jump around," said Mr. Panayiotou. "You sort of get used to that feeling of trying hard but being unable to do it. You feel stupid, even though you think that you are smart but just cannot prove it.

"I can read better now because I've memorised a lot of words, but when I get to surnames and words I've never seen, it's nigh on impossible. When I drive on the motorway, I have to concentrate to read the road signs. It still induces feelings of anxiety. Filling out forms for stuff like passport control is also a no-go area."

How has he managed to overcome this handicap and become so successful?

"The flip side of dyslexia is that you develop other gifts. I've trained my mind to have a photographic memory. I have a phenomenal memory. It also makes you more creative in solving problems because your mind is always in a fight to comprehend the world around you. It's always fighting, fighting, fighting. That makes you stronger because you learn to handle problems as part of life.

"It also makes you super-focused. I can tell you where every suit in my wardrobe is, every car in my garage, I can remember the profit figure on a hotel I was told about three months ago. You learn to simplify things, to get to the bottom line which is good for business and decision-making.

"With me, my desk, my wardrobe, my day - it's all regimented. I'm up at 7 am, I walk the Dobermann, I'm out of the house by 8.30 am, at work an hour later, then at 5 pm I go to the gym. Every day it's the same."

He added: "I don't want to give the impression that being dyslexic is a ticket to success, because it isn't, but with the right attitude, it can be overcome. In my case, it gave me a burning desire to prove myself.

"It's no coincidence that I took up boxing at seven, the same age my teacher shamed me. I became known as the hardest kid in the school. I was kicked out of high school for laying out the PE teacher with a punch when I was 14. I never went back. If you can't read or write, there's no point being there."

The following year, Mr. Panayiotou became the Essex under-16 amateur middleweight boxing champion and went to work for his father. The first book he ever read was at 17: "I was passionate about getting my pilot's licence and I memorised the entire manual."

A few years later he bought a small property in Islington, converted it into flats, and started what would become one of the biggest buy-to-let empires in Britain. In 2007 he sold thousands of flats, focusing instead on building a portfolio of hotels.

His firm, The Ability Group, now has seven. His latest development, the £70million Waldorf-Astoria, has just opened at Syon Park. He is about to put "Britain's most expensive house" on the market - a redeveloped property in The Bishop's Avenue in Hampstead, which he hopes to sell for £100million.

Mr. Panayiotou comes from poor parents who couldn't speak or read English, but he thinks immigrant children with their drive to succeed can overcome these obstacles. His older brother George came from the same background as him, he points out, yet did well at school and completed a business degree.

"I think I would have benefited from an early diagnosis of my problem by my teachers," he said. "Our daughter Sofia is 12 and has dyslexia. My wife got her a diagnosis and brilliant specialized tutor from age six. She would draw a cat and write "cat" under it and Sofia would memorise it. Her problem was named and she was given the skills to master it.

"My wife also spends a lot of time reading with her. Sofia has been trained from an early age to memorise whole words, and now she reads fine and is doing fantastically at school."

Mr. Panayiotou says that being unable to read today is far more devastating than in the Seventies. "Although I have been successful beyond my dreams, jobs are a lot more sophisticated than they were 30 years ago, and technology. I would hate for any child to have to go through what I did.

"Your illiteracy campaign can make a difference to kids like me. Being able to read is as fundamental as eating. You can't get by without knowing how to read."

*   *   *

After I read this article, I decided I wanted to meet him and transform his lifelong challenge with reading by teaching him our Universal Reading Method. I attempted to call him and sent him an email outlining how we could arrange to teach him to read.

Approximately two weeks after I read the article in the *Evening Standard* and attempted to reach Mr. Panayiotou, a friend of mine, Emily Primrose Brown, a teacher in London, contacted me and told me that she had been contacted by a mother of a challenged reader who wanted to provide me with airfare to London and pay me to teach her son how to read, and other students as well. I was delighted because Emily and her family offered to let their adopted "Uncle Craig" stay at their flat with them while I was teaching.

I am always surprised when what I am manifesting seems to appear on the scene. So here I was with Mr. Panayiotou in my sights and I was now on my way to London with a strong intention to meet him and teach him to read.

. When I arrived in London, I first fulfilled my promises to Emily. I enjoyed teaching the young man to whom Emily had introduced me. His parents were from Ghana, and I also delighted in teaching his cousin. I successfully taught another student whose parents were from India.

Next, after experiencing challenges getting an appointment with Mr. Panayiotou by calling his office, I decided to go to his office and see if I could meet him early in the morning just before he walked into his building. When I went to the listed address the night before, so I would know where I was going, I found they had just recently relocated their offices. After a little inquiring, I found his new address. It was like I was in my investigator mode again, skip-tracking someone.

The next day I waited 2 1/2 hours at the new address for Mr. Panayiotou to arrive. It was brisk and raining that morning. I felt like Sherlock Holmes or someone from Scotland Yard on a stake-out. I was wearing my trench coat and a wool hat. So, I quite fit the part.

As I stood there waiting for him, I kept looking at the picture that I had copied from the article so when he arrived I would recognize him. According to the article in the *Evening Standard*, he was quoted as saying, "I always arrive at work at 9:00 am." I wanted to be sure not to miss him; I arrived at 8:00 am.

However, this day was not a normal day for Mr. Panayiotou. I learned later that he had an appointment out of the office. So, it appeared I had no other choice than to speak to the Security Guard at the lower entrance of the building and ask him to connect me with his assistant whom I had spoken to before from San Diego. Using the Security Office phone, I spoke briefly with his assistant and asked her to have him call me, politely reminding her that she and I had spoken before.

I then went to turn on my mobile phone in order to receive any incoming calls, especially from Mr. Panayiotou, only to discover that my phone was not working. A little rattled, I walked quickly a couple of doors down the street to a mobile phone store to see if they could fix it.

It was something simple and took very little time to fix. As I exited the phone store to return to the street, I was absolutely amazed that there in front of me was the man in the picture that I had been looking at all morning, Andreas Panayiotou.

I immediately reached out my hand and introduced myself. "I am Craig Collins. I have been trying to reach you by phone for several weeks. I have a miracle to share with you. I have come all the way from California to teach you how to read and I can do so in just one 2 1/2-hour session!"

OK, I said it! Holding my breath and feeling my heart beating, I waited for him to respond.

After looking at me for a short time, then to his left side, our hands still clasped in our shake, he quietly spoke to me. "How come you did not make an appointment with my assistant?"

I responded, "I tried, several times, but your assistant was not too keen on the idea. So, I just knew I had to talk to you!"

"I was not going to be in the office today, but I forgot some important papers I needed for my meeting, and I never forget anything! I would not be here if I hadn't forgotten them," he said.

Looking off to the left, as if in thought, he pondered my statement and finally responded.

"Yes, I will meet with you and I will have my assistant contact you and tell you the date and time," Andreas Panayiotou stated. I was absolutely in bliss.

It was the morning of November 8th, 2011 when I returned to the front of the same office building where I had stood days earlier. I walked through the large doors and announced proudly to the Security Guard that I was there for an appointment with Andreas Panayiotou. He made a phone call and I was told to wait. Natalie, Andreas' assistant, was coming down. I thought, how nice, must be a high security office and she needs to escort me upstairs.

I was wrong and could feel this in the pit of my stomach, as I listened to Natalie, with her cheerful smile, apologize.

"Andy has been called away for an emergency meeting." She went on to say, "If you ever return to London, please let us know and possibly he will be able to see you then."

My heart sank as I looked at her, returning her smile, and confidently responded:

"When I spoke to Mr. Panayiotou, I told him I would cancel my return flight to San Diego to meet with him and that I had a place to stay with a friend. So, I won't be leaving and can easily be available any time for him to meet with me."

As she walked towards the elevator she looked back and assured me, "I will pass on your message to Mr. Panayiotou."

I must say, I am not sure if his assistant was pleased that I had met Mr. Panayiotou on the street and that he had made plans to meet with me. She saw me as a solicitor, and it was her job to keep people from reaching him.

I was deeply disappointed. I was afraid Mr. Panayiotou would not call me back and I would miss this "window of opportunity" to teach this famous man to read.

Based on Karma—I am from California—it just didn't make sense that I wouldn't get to transform him. So, as I rode one of London's red double decker buses to my friend Sally's flat on Abbey Road where I was now staying, I went over everything again in my mind.

I had read the article about him in the *London Evening Standard* on the computer in San Diego. I had received a free flight to London. I had two delightful friends who invited me to stay with them at their flat. I had the foresight to go the night before to locate his office. I found the new address without having to compromise the time I needed to show up at his office early in the morning. And, of all the miracles, I unexpectedly ran into him in front of the phone store and he said, "Yes, I will meet with you."

So, I had to believe I would hear from him when he returned to his office, but my confidence was shaken.

When I arrived back at Sally's flat, which was connected to St. John's Wood Baptist Church, the first parish where church members were taught to read in order to read the Bible, we decided to go to a movie while I waited for Mr. Panayiotou to call.

At the theatre, I was required to turn off my phone before entering. The man at the door actually turned it off for me. Without my phone available I walked into the theatre in somewhat of a daze and sat down.

Feeling anxious and distracted from the movie, I was equally annoyed when a cell phone went off somewhere in the theatre. Looking around for the offender I happened to notice a light shining through my coat pocket and was able to locate the ringing phone. It was my phone ringing. My heart began to race!

I grabbed my coat trying to muffle the ring and hurried out of the theatre through the front doors. The light outside of the theatre, even in the rain, made it possible for me to see that the call was from Natalie. I answered, trying to sound casual, and listened to her providing me a new date and time to meet with Mr. Panayiotou. I felt both relieved and elated.

The date and time of our new meeting was November 11, 2011 at 1:30 pm. (11-11-11) What an amazing omen; this was the date when I was to teach Mr. Panayiotou to read.

I arrived early for our meeting. While waiting in the outer office to meet with Mr. Panayiotou, I read an article about him in a local business magazine. The more I read the more I was impressed with this man and realized I was in the sacred space of someone very powerful. Everyone in the office was entrusted with keeping him safe and protecting him from intrusion and I was sitting in his waiting room. I had made it past the first wall and was on my way into the inner sanctum.

After a short while, Natalie ushered me into his office. I was now in the inner sanctuary of Andreas Panayiotou, whom I had taken on the task to transform his deepest shame into his greatest asset.

I viewed what seemed to be a silver throne to the right of the entrance as I walked on black and white marble squares. I sat down across from him at his black desk.

"I am being polite to see you because you have come so far to meet me," Mr. Panayiotou announced formally. "What is the purpose of your wanting to meet with me?"

Surprised by his question, my response was still confident and resolute.

"I have come here to share a miracle with you and teach you how to read English. I only need a couple of hours of your time."

After a thoughtful pause and again looking off to the left, as he did when I met him on the street, as if someone was talking to him, he stood up and declared:

"OK, then, let's do it!"

So, I helped him clear off the end of his long black marble conference table and I laid out the two plastic covered sheets of paper on which was printed our entire Universal Reading Method. As we sat down, I was still fearful that he might change his mind, so I immediately began with asking him to read some words on our pre-test. It was clear what he had said in the article was true. He could not read.

Then I began the instruction.

I explained to him, "I am going to ask you a question that I do not want you to answer. I just want you to listen to the question and ponder the answer I provide you." He nodded affirmatively.

"What does your mouth do when you read?" I inquired. "Your mouth opens and closes, doesn't it? And it makes sounds."

After about five minutes and having taught him the first two concepts, Mr. Panayiotou abruptly stood up and walked back to his desk, lifted the mouth piece off of his phone, and spoke into it.

"Hold all of my calls and cancel all of my appointments for the rest of the afternoon." I had been formally announced and accepted to teach my student to read.

When he returned to his chair, he smiled at me and then nodded for me to proceed. I repeated the first two concepts for him and continued to teach him the rest of our Universal Reading Method from where we left off.

Mr. Panayiotou learned in 30 minutes what normally takes students one hour. He was a very focused person and when he gave his full attention it was intense. At the end of 30 minutes, he read a 29-letter, nine-syllable fictitious word that we have created that cannot be read without having learned the first six of the seven concepts.

Since there were no words that long that he knew or had ever read in his whole vocabulary, he was quite impressed that he was able to read such a word. I would say the look on his face was a mixture of shock and excitement.

I, too, was quite impressed because, with all due respect, Mr.

Panayiotou had left school at the age of 14 and was from a family where the primary language was Greek. He was not familiar with the basics of reading English words.

Andreas Panayiotou's courage and absolute focus on my every word, coupled with our teaching him just seven concepts, invited him to realize that he now had the tools necessary to read every English word he came across, for the first time ever, in his life.

During the 15-minute break we stood outside on a patio that was attached to his office and enjoyed the cool air. Mr. Panayiotou took some quiet time from my instruction to consolidate the information he had just received.

Returning inside, I handed him the four printed, plastic-covered sheets of paper that I had taught him from before his break. I instructed Mr. Panayiotou to review the information on his own for another 15 minutes. He diligently studied the seven concepts from the plastic-covered sheets. Exactly 15 minutes later, he announced to me:

"I completely understand this!"

During the second half of our session Mr. Panayiotou learned all the exceptions, again, in one-half hour, not the full hour in which we usually teach them. After we finished with the instruction, I realized why Andreas Panayiotou was successful. I believe he was and always has been an incredibly brilliant and focused man. I could not help but reflect on what it must have been like for him to know he could not read; and I so admired him for making his statement to the newspaper and for committing his time to me today.

After we completed the learning sessions, including the 15 minutes of consolidation time and review, I removed from my backpack a list of 475 multi-syllable college-level words from the California GED. On this list are words that he had never seen before and would not have attempted in the past.

When he finished reading aloud all the multi-syllable words correctly on the first page, I said, "Please read the next page of words a little faster!"

He responded, "Faster?"

I nodded. So, he cleared his throat, looked at the next page and began to read them . . . faster. It was obvious he had a very large verbal and listening vocabulary.

He commented, "I know these words, I just didn't know what they looked like on a printed page."

There were three-, four-, and five-syllable sophisticated words, and after just 1 1/2 hours of my instructing him, including the 15 minutes he spent on the patio and the 15-minute review, Mr. Panayiotou was impressively reading and comprehending all the words on all of the pages. He had learned to read faster than anyone I have ever taught and that is still true today.

While he was checking his phone messages I walked into his outer office and picked up the magazine I had been reading while waiting to meet with him. I brought it back into his office, closing the door, and offered the article for him to read, aloud.

After reading several paragraphs, he exclaimed, putting his finger on the paragraph to save his place, "This is an article about me!"

He then read the rest of the article that was two columns and took up the whole page, approximately 12 paragraphs long.

When Mr. Panayiotou finished reading and comprehending the whole article, he stood up, faced me, and proclaimed enthusiastically, "I want to teach the whole world how to read English, not just England, the whole world, with your reading method!"

While looking over the list of words he had just read, he looked up at me and said, "I think your reading method is something you should share with Sir Richard Branson. He is holding a business conference at one of my hotels soon! I believe he would be very interested!" Mr. Panayiotou added.

"I've received more calls about my article in the *London Evening Standard* than I have ever received regarding any of the projects I have completed or hotels I have built." He further shared with me, "One of them was from Queen Elizabeth. She asked me what my next step was. I told her I didn't know what my next step would be."

Then he looked up at me and said, "Now, I do!"

I must share something with you. There were times in this business when I was ahead of myself. At the time of teaching Mr. Panayiotou, the only thing I had to offer was me and, on a few pages of paper, my brother's method to teach someone to read in record time, and the kindness of friends and volunteers to support my doing so.

We had not begun producing our promotional presentation video which told our story and we had just begun to collect evidence about the numbers of students we had taught. We had not yet created our Universal Reading Method video or online instruction either. Over the next year, however, we produced a truly exceptional, professional, and informative promotional video.

Reflecting on that time, I realized that it was with Andreas Panayiotou I learned that being able to read and being intelligent have nothing to do with each other. Mr. Panayiotou had always been brilliant, he just didn't know how to read. Now he did and has continued to be a shining star in the hotel business world.

As I continued to visit cities in different places in the world, I realized our success with teaching Andreas Panayiotou to read is one that can be achieved by every person to whom we teach our Universal Reading Method, as long as they do not have a hearing or vision issue, nor taking some sort of drugs.

When we are attempting to overcome the *status quo,* we are led in many directions and have to trust everything is happening for the "right" reason. In my world, on my way to teach the entire world to read English, there are many events that take place that are definitely not "My will be done!" So, with each detour on the road, I say, "I will Thy will be done" . . . immediately after I stop gritting my teeth.

Chapter 6

The Road To Our Online Course Via Skype. Aloha!

Matai

While in San Diego, I was contacted by Shelly Seleni, the mother of a young Samoan boy, Matai, who asked me to teach her son to read on Skype. After sending her our 5-page Teaching Guide, our Pre-test, and five pages of multi-syllable words, we arranged to contact on Skype.

We learned a great deal by teaching our Universal Reading Method on Skype. We learned that the student stops focusing on me, his instructor, and focuses exclusively on learning to read and the instruction.

The student focuses on the papers before him while listening to an audio instruction. Like in a video game, the student does not have to worry about thoughts and feelings for the instructor. *Do I like him? Does he like me? What do I think of him? Do I think he is dumb? Does he think I am dumb?* etc. In other words, no extra distractions.

While being on the other side of the camera with Matai I was provided this incredible insight. Now we know what our students will experience when learning from our online Universal Reading Method and the success they will have when there is not an instructor in the room to divert their attention. At the same time the delivery is made by a recording that is always supportive and non-judgmental.

Matai actually forgot I was there and when I told him it was time for him to take his break and walk around the block, he looked up at the screen for the first time and looked surprised to see me. I think, with the advent of computer games, young people are conditioned to interact with just a computer and not people, so interacting with me on Skype was similar.

After Matai learned to read and successfully read all five pages of our multi-syllable words, while Shellie sat in a chair behind him listening intently and in disbelief, she wrote to us on Facebook the following:

"Today I witnessed a breakthrough in reading with Matai. After being told that Matai was dyslexic and may be held back if he

couldn't read at a certain "speed," Matai and I fought back. Speed? Really?

What happened to comprehension? I don't care if you can read a thousand words per minute, if you don't understand what you're reading, what good will that do for you? It won't!!!

I know my son's comprehension and articulation surpasses kids much older than him. He is so intelligent, and I just needed to find a way to get him reading at the same level as his speech and comprehension level.

Enter Craig Collins and the Universal Reading Method. In 3 hours via Skype, I watched my son start the process reading very VERY choppy . . . to reading 3- to 6-syllable words at a college level with confidence and ease.

Not perfect, but he knew how and where to adjust sounds. And because his vocabulary is so vast, he was able to not only say the words . . . he understood them.

Then he read from the first page of the book Spirit Animals *with such ease that what normally would have taken him five minutes, he read in less than a minute.*

As much as I wanted to cry with joy, I knew it was more important to just CELEBRATE MATAI!!! I am so excited for him and the endless possibilities and opportunities that he is already and will be able to explore.

Thank you so much, Craig, for your time and patience. I watched a burden lift from my son that no one can ever put back on him. WE ARE FOREVER GRATEFUL!

If you know anyone ages 5 to 95 challenged with reading, in-

box me; we will be hosting reading workshops on Oahu and Maui so let me know and I'll make sure to get you in with Craig while he's here.

Exciting times ahead for keiki o ka aina . . . CheeeHoooo, "

Shelly Seleni

With each student I taught, I learned that no matter if we were teaching on Skype, or me in person, or eventually on our video, it is the concepts my brother created for the Universal Reading Method that provide the amazing reading transformation in such a short span of time.

We can now reach millions of students all over the world. We have broken the code to learning to read and now reading is available to everyone, not just the select few.

Chapter 7

We Are Online

Populations-of-the-world challenged with reading English have been told, and believe, that English is a very hard language to learn to read. The truth is – it is not!

We had been attracting students and personally transforming them from significantly challenged readers to confident and competent readers for about a year in California. I was teaching them one-on-one, but to reach the populations that could not read English in the world we were going to have to expand our method of teaching, we were going to have to provide a Universal Reading Method video and train affiliates to provide it to individuals and classes of students. We needed to provide our instruction online so that anyone with a computer or iPad could "help themselves to learning to read" at their own convenience.

Because of my success with teaching Matai on Skype, I knew I no longer needed to be a "real person." I could be an online instructor!

It soon became obvious, that teaching with our video and graduating to our online Universal Reading Method would provide our students with a clearer path to learning to read, with much less intimidation.

In the United States there are 90+ million adults who are functionally illiterate, according to the published study on Literacy in

America by the National Commission on Adult Literacy (2008) *Reach Higher, America: Overcoming Crisis in the US Workforce.* [Internet] Council for Advancement of Adult Literacy. Available from: http://www.nationalcommissiononadultliteracy.org/report.html

We had two feelings; we were both concerned because the numbers were staggering, and we were excited because we knew we had the solution. I was told by a community college administrator that 51% of the students who are leaving high school, including those who are graduating, are reading at a 4th grade level and that many of those students are ending up in jail or prison because they do not qualify to continue their education in a community college.

Then I started asking friends I knew: "When you read, how do you know when a vowel is long or short?" Often their response was, "I memorized it, I don't know why!" Then I told them our magic solution and they got it immediately. You have memorized the words you read and you sometimes have no idea how to pronounce a word you "don't know." Well, after you learn the Universal Reading Method there no more "don't know" words.

Another clue I provided to our Miracle Readers is I would tell them my 10-digit telephone number, which included my area code, and asked them to repeat it for me. Everyone asked me to repeat it and wanted to write it down. However, when I told them my 7-digit phone number, without the three extra digits in the area code, they, smiling, easily repeated it. We teach seven concepts. Research tells us that seven is the optimum number of concepts that most people can retain. We are obsessed with making sure that we only teach our students seven concepts and our obsession is really paying off.

Imagine you are one of our affiliate instructors and you have been witnessing student after student learning to read from just 2 1/2 hours of instruction from a video. I became very encouraged to make our Universal Reading Method available to more people. So, we decided to film me teaching on camera and create our first prototype of our Universal Reading Method video.

On one of the few rainy days in San Diego, Ron Franklin, our Software Engineer and the narrator of our Presentation video, and I were sitting in a charter school classroom with four classes of 39 fifth-, sixth-, seventh- and eighth-grade students from a cross-section of foreign countries. Our students were from families whose parents barely spoke English and the students had been tested and were found to be reading significantly below their grade level. (They were reading small words and very few, if any, multi-syllable words.)

After we received the invitation to teach this challenging group of students and having taught several students on Skype, we decided to teach the four classes with a video of me teaching instead of my personally teaching them. It was time to find out if we could teach larger numbers of students in many different locations at the same time, and with a video instead of a teacher.

As Ron and I sat to the side of the class of students as they watched our video, we sat excited, anticipating that our video would achieve the goals we had set for these students over a two-day period. It was definitely challenging giving up my control of being the teacher and, as the video progressed, we became excited with how well the students participated and responded.

Ron and I were both impressed that we were capturing all the students' attention with our video instruction. Our concern was about the "rough-draft" appearance of our video and that sometimes the words did not match up with the graphics on the screen, this being our first video experiment with several classes of learners.

After about an hour of video instruction, we directed the students to take a 15-minute walk, go outside, have some water, not open their cell phones, and return for a review of the information that was presented on the video from our four-page handout. From teaching our prior students we have learned this is when everything begins to get clear for them, a time of consolidation takes place.

As the learners filed back into class and studied on their own for 15 minutes and then went back to the video to learn the exceptional sounds, both Ron and I observed with anticipation just how many students would receive our instruction and transform into a confident, competent reader.

So here is what we discovered:

After the students completed watching the last concept in our video, we broke each class up into two teams with equal numbers of students on each team. Then we gave a five-page list of multi-syllable words, 475 words from the GED, all post high school words, to each person in the class.

The teacher from our first class had shared with us who her most challenged students were.

We started with the team to the left, knowing that the challenged students were the second group of five, all in row. As we went back and forth between teams, we were impressed that each of these first students read ALL the words on all five pages.

When we got to the identified "most challenged" students, we asked them to read the words. Each of the challenged students started off slowly and with hesitation. However, since we were patient with them and reminded them of the four key concepts they could use to read the words, all of a sudden each of the "most challenged" —like a light went on—began to read the words. I am an emotional person and each time this happens it gives me chills.

After the identified students who were slower than the rest read all the words, I watched the rest of the class revisiting our review sheets and looking at their own list of words in preparation for their turn at reading those same words.

They definitely knew the students who had just succeeded were identified as the 'dummies' in their class by their teacher, and realized that if they couldn't succeed, they would be taking their place. It was significant to watch as I saw them get serious about learning from our instruction.

At the end of each of the four class instructions, all the students—100 % of the them—read all 475 words from the five pages of college- level words. I was very impressed and happy to see this. Especially since this first video was so poorly edited.

Each time another class of students came in, I went through my doubts that it would work with all of the students. After all, they were from different countries. In the beginning, we started with 5th graders and finished with the 8th graders. At the end of each class, during our 475-word reading game, I was pleasantly surprised with the accuracy and fluency they were able to read the words. It is times like this when my heart races and I realize, even more, the impact we will have as our instruction reaches the masses of challenged readers in the world.

Both Ron Franklin and I were absolutely amazed at the success these four classes of students had. It meant that we now could further fine-tune our Universal Reading Method video.

When we returned to our office, Doug viewed our current video and added additional wording that made the instruction clearer and Ron Franklin worked diligently to make everything in sync.

We set out to create the perfect remedial reading instruction that has become our online Universal Reading Method and is now available to everyone, without the need for an instructor. We had discovered something very significant.

Since then, our Universal Reading Method video has been successfully tested with several hundred students and presented by several of our Affiliates with documented success. Affiliates are people who have joined our team because they have been transformed or have witnessed someone else be transformed by the reading program and are passionate about helping people become readers.

Because of the success of our online instruction, we can now provide our Universal Reading Method to both individuals and classes and reach millions of students all over the world.

Chapter 8

Chicago, A place to Start Our Worldwide Universal Reading Method Literacy Tour

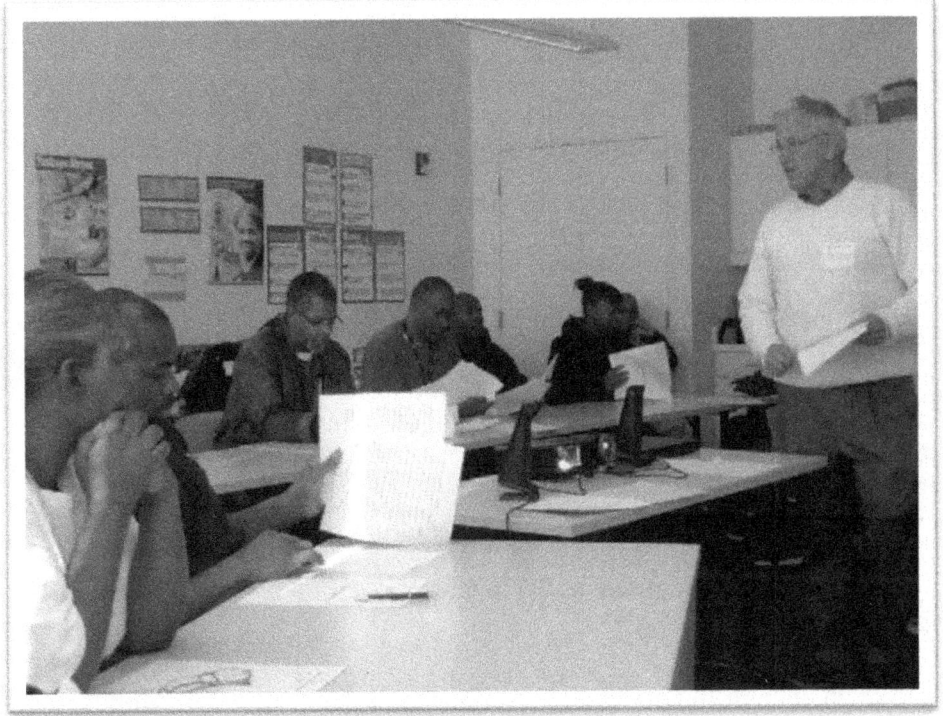

Craig Collins Teaching Learners, in Chicago at A Safe Haven™

As I stood in line, waiting to board "standby" on a United Airlines flight to Chicago, Illinois, I reflected on my fun meeting with a woman named Carol who had volunteered to host me in her home and introduce me to students in Chicago who have difficulty with reading English. I was looking forward to meeting her husband and her family. It promised to be a full house and a very new experience for me. My brother left home when I was twelve years old, so I was kind of an only child and did not have any children of my own.

I was on an exciting adventure and feeling very confident about meeting and bringing a transformation with our Universal Reading Method to many new challenged readers I have never met before. I was in search of the evidence that will help describe us as an "Evidenced-Based Reading Method."

The "Windy City" was just that—a big city that I had never met before. When I stood in the street downtown, the wind whipped around the tall buildings and almost knocked me over.

My California desire to sit on a beach and take in the beauty of a body of water was satisfied by walking along the edge of Lake Michigan with my friend Ulwyn and enjoying a nap under a tree. Navy Pier was really fun with its giant Ferris Wheel which took me high in the sky to enjoy the moon shining on the water.

There were many parks in Chicago and they often had lakes. I visited one where the rocks were believed to be healing rocks and part of an ancient Indian healing ground. In fact, one of the healing rocks from that lake was deposited in the front yard of a place I was hosted. When I mowed the lawn, I used to lay on it and meditate. Whenever I got the chance, I enjoyed pruning, trimming and making my new friend's yard beautiful. Getting enough exercise was always my challenge.

Wherever we went, Carol and I were excellent at speaking with strangers and invited them to make an appointment to learn to read with me at the local library. We were quite the dynamic duo. We spoke at Rotary Clubs and Chamber of Commerce meetings and Carol set up a booth at a weekend conference while I gave talks about our Universal Reading Method. I felt well received and Carol's outgoing manner generated many appointments for successful teaching experiences.

One very engaging experience we had with A Safe haven, a homeless facility on Chicago's West Side, comes to my mind. Carol and I just walked in and made an appointment to meet with their CEO after meeting with one of the people who was on their board of directors.

After meeting with the CEO/Manager Brian Rowland and staff at A Safe Haven, it was decided that they would allow us to teach about 20 of their residents who were having difficulty with reading English, with the intention to see if we could bring our Universal Reading Method to their approximately 1,200 residents per year.

During the staff meeting I explained that students are taught just once, and for 2 ½ hours, and that at the end of that time each student would increase their reading ability by a minimum of two grade levels but often more, since at the end of the session, we have each student read several hundred college-level multi-syllable words.

A real concern expressed by the paid teachers at A Safe Haven during an introductory meeting was: "What will we do with a student when they have learned to read in just 2 ½ hours? Most of what we do is try to teach our residents to read. We won't know what to do with them."

I suggested, "Teach them to fill out a job application, write a story, write a play, enter classes at a training school or community college, and/or qualify for a job that requires reading." I was surprised that some of the teachers were not in favor of us teaching the residents.

After a private session with Brian Roland, it was decided that he would authorize our pre-testing some of the residence of A Safe Haven, providing them with instruction from our Universal Reading Method video, and guiding them through an exercise where they would read from a five-page list of college level words after viewing and speaking along with the video.

This was a very exciting moment for us. Remember, I am traveling at this time to research and provide evidence-based experiences and results with the diverse group of students we are transforming into readers. I have just been welcomed to teach homeless adult men and women to read, some who have an ankle bracelet on that signifies that some of them are prisoners who are still in jail.

Later, this opened up an opportunity to meet a group of folks who worked with and provided services at other halfway houses for folks who had been in jail and prison and possibly provide our instruction to inmates at the jail.

Carol, another Chicago friend of mine named Jay, and I left early the morning we were scheduled to teach the residents and drove back to the West Side of Chicago to A Safe Haven. As we sat in the car waiting for the big hand to reach the 12 so we could enter the facility, we exchanged supportive words that would help us to feel calm during our session. It was decided that we would each pre-test 1/3 of the class using the WRAT 3, so we could begin our instruction as soon as possible.

We had a total of 15 students that were chosen by the teachers at A Safe Haven to attend our class. Each student was required to read as many as possible of the 42 words from one sheet of paper. The purpose of the pre-test was to establish each student's level of reading and to inform us as well.

As Carol, Jay and I pre-tested the students it became clear that we had four students who were challenged with reading both the mono- and multi-syllable words, reading at approximately a 3rd to 4th grade level, and six of the residents were able to read by sight the mono-syllable words but could not read any of the multi-syllable words.

So, we had 10 or 15 target students plus five students who were able to read both the mono and multi-syllable words on the pre-test. I decided to allow them to stay because of the other benefits our students receive when we expose them to our Universal Reading Method.

Of interest, one of the women, a woman I pre-tested with the CEO Brian Roland sitting next to me, was having audio hallucinations and "talking to her voices" and was not in contact.

At first, I was tempted to ask her to leave, then remembered the training I received while working on a locked unit of a mental hospital. I was working on my master's degree in Psychiatric Social Work at the time, so at that moment I turned to her and said, "I am glad you are here. I want you to stay. Your talking to your voices will interrupt other people. Can you ask your voices to leave you alone for a couple of hours and not talk to them?"

I wish I could describe the look on her face. She thought about it for a moment and then said, "Yes!" For the rest of the instruction, she followed along with the class and did not make one inappropriate comment.

Although she was unable to read one word on the pre-test, I believe because of her no longer being distracted with her hallucination, when it came time to read the words from our multi-syllable word list, she read all of them.

Brian Roland listened to her intently and when he addressed the class at the end he spoke from his heart and appeared to be quite moved by what he had observed. Watching 15 people read 475 multi-syllable words is quite impressive, especially when two thirds of them were only reading at a 4th grade level just 2 ½ hours earlier.

After the class was over, I walked over to the woman who had been hearing voices. Looking into her eyes and receiving full contact, I told her I felt she should try taking a few classes at a community college because of how well she was reading.

As I spoke, her eyes focused on mine; I could see the tears welling up around her eyes, still in focus. As the tears fell down her cheeks, she whispered to me, "I am crying because no one has ever told me anything like that. Do you think I am smart enough?"

I responded, "Yes, you just read several pages of large college words!"

At the end of the class, only two people did not read the words. One who refused to and, after Carol spoke to him and regained his confidence, later changed his mind and read the words; and one who did not know the alphabet and, giving me a big hug, told me that he thought he might read some day. He did read several words from our list.

One of the challenges I have experienced is that decisions are not being made based on what would be best for the challenged readers, be it a homeless facility like A Safe Haven or a public school. Politics appear to play a big part in the decisions and will have a long term and significant impact on these folk's quality of life.

I was very proud and pleased as I listened to 15 students read five pages of multi-syllable words, especially those ten who had difficulty with the pre-test. I loved the positive comments at the end from the CEO and several of the teachers who were sitting in the classroom observing. It was an obvious win/win for everyone that day.

During the next couple of weeks, a friend of Carol's, Wayne Anderson, put together an excellent fundraising video for us to use with A Safe Haven to raise money to implement our Universal Reading Method and teach it to all the residents.

However, despite all of our success, a decision was made not to follow through with implementing the Universal Reading Method at their facility.

When we perfect our online Universal Reading Method, maybe A Safe Haven will change their mind. It certainly would be a happy day for the residents who live there.

Soon after A Safe Haven, I gave a presentation to about 15 people at a friend of Carol's beauty shop. One of the people who was attracted to learning to read was Patricia. At one point, because of her fear, she walked out to leave, and Carol had to convince her to return. However, by the end of the presentation, she consented to being taught and we drove to her home.

At her kitchen table, I taught Patricia our Universal Reading Method while Carol sat quietly observing.

Within the 2 ½ hour-period that I taught her, Patricia was not only reading from a list of college words, but her whole affect changed. It was as if she matured from a young-acting person into a mature adult. It was very impressive. Carol was truly amazed, and I felt watching this student's immediate and truly significant transformation helped Carol to garner the excellent support she manifested during my maiden voyage to Chicago.

Over the next several months, I witnessed Patricia change the way she dressed, participate in the adult world at a business club she belonged to, receive compliments from her friends, and successfully have a holiday party at her home where people had such a good time they did not want to leave.

It was very rewarding to see the transformation of Patricia and as I think of her while writing, I am smiling and sending her supportive thoughts and appreciation for the courageous, kind, and dear person she is.

In Chicago I learned so much, I matured in a way that helped me to make decisions about our Literacy Tour that increased our success and improved our relationships with all whom we were meeting there and in other areas.

I am sincerely appreciative of the support I received from everyone I met and who helped us to receive the positive experience we had teaching our students.

If it hadn't been for the excellent coaching I was receiving from Dr. Ulwyn Pierre, I would have probably returned home instead of continuing my tour into Canada, onto New York, and across the pond to Scotland and England. Never underestimate the power of friendships and good sound advice.

As I boarded the Amtrak train for the second time, leaving Chicago to travel to upstate New York, I looked out the window and said goodbye, remembering the many people I had met, spent time with, and taught to read. As I settled into my seat, I looked around me and said hello to the next leg of my adventure. I just adored trains and this one looked like it was going to be a fun ride.

"All Aboard!"

Chapter 9

All Aboard the Reading Train

"My heart is warm with the friends I make
And better friend I'll not be knowing,
Yet there isn't a train I wouldn't take
No matter where it is going."
  Edna St. Vincent Millay

Trains fascinate me. They seem to be spontaneous little communities with many stories that come together settled in small cars. On trains people speak to one another. We travelers are unique people who love the newness of our every day and the people in it. When you travel by train you are carried away in the motion, the rocking back and forth, and the sound of the clack, clack, clack of the metal wheels on the track. When you look outside, especially in the night, towns and cities are passing by without stories or mention. The capsule our lives are contained in is our train car and is our whole world during that time.

I met many wonderful people on the train from Chicago to Toronto; three stand out. Two became students, people who could not afford to pay but were sponsored by my Angels who provided scholarships for them.

One of my students was a delightful 50-year-old woman who was traveling from California to Boston to see her daughter for

Christmas. She told me our reading experience changed her life, and this touched me deeply. Another was a man who was heading to Montreal to receive a promotion in a construction company where he worked. I taught him with our video. When he arrived for his interview, he aced the written test part of it because he could now read. He called me to thank me right after the interview. It was truly gratifying to have this miracle flow through me to the not-so-random folks I was meeting. They both had a secret when they got on the train and when they got off their secret about not being able to read was gone.

The third person, Nathan Minnehan, a true Renaissance Man on his way to New York to see his family for Christmas, become my soul-brother and forever friend. He is a poet, a troubadour, a keynote speaker, the owner of Walk & Talk Marketing, and a delightful man with many talents. We have stayed in touch while he traveled to the Czech Republic and Portugal and I have traveled across the United States, into Canada, to the UK and back, and to Hawaii. We have stayed friends ever since.

When I arrived in Quebec, I visited a close French-speaking friend of mine, Louis Guy. Quebec was very picturesque. I rode my bike along the shore of the St. Lawrence River and got to have my first experience of "the first day of winter." I learned about frost bite and how to walk my bike when traveling into the wind so that you don't freeze. We made many wonderful meals and I so welcomed having a brother in Quebec. After a short while, the more I practiced speaking French, the more I could understand the news in French and speak easier with Louis Guy.

Louis Guy had traveled back and forth to China as a college professor and during my stay introduced me to some Chinese friends. That's when I discovered that Chinese people have the same positive experience learning to read with our Universal Reading Method video as do the English-speaking folks. It was very revealing for me and opened a whole other part of the world of students for us. There is a huge desire on the part of Chinese families for their children to become fluent in English.

Next stop Toronto.

Chapter 10

A Star is Born

"Parents can only give good advice or put them on the right paths, but the final forming of a person's character lies in their own hands."

Anne Frank

It was early November 2013 and very cold, without much snow. I had never been to Toronto before, and, for that matter, never rode overnight on a train. Once there, I was driven out of town to visit with my close friend, Christina Reeves, for a few days. It was great to see her, and I had a fun time teaching both of her grandchildren with our Universal Reading Method video. I still love receiving word from Grammy Christina about the academic achievements of her grandchildren.

Returning to Toronto I had been invited to stay in the beautiful condo of Anand Murthy and his delightful wife above Lake Ontario. The view from Anand's condo, of Ward Island during the early morning sunrise with the Ferry Crossing and a plane preparing for landing at the nearby Ontario airport, was spectacular. I felt like a king when I was staying at their place. Anand is a gentleman's gentleman, a deeply spiritual man and businessman who loaned us some money to help us in the marketing of our reading program. I hope to repay him soon for his kindness and generosity.

While in Toronto, I received the opportunity to teach Josh

Niedermayer, the son of the famous hockey player, Scott Niedermayer, who was receiving the WHL award the same weekend I was there. It was quite a coincidence since they lived in Southern California and, at that time, I did not call any place my home.

As I got all bundled up in my snow parka, gloves, boots, and two sweaters and walked from the condo to the nearby hotel, about five blocks along the river, I couldn't have been more excited to be on my way to teaching this young man and enjoying the cold.

As planned, I met Josh with his mom in the lobby of the hotel. After a brief introduction and while many members of the family were celebrating the achievements of his dad, Josh, his mother Lisa, a favorite uncle and I escaped into one of the hotel rooms upstairs, reserved for the family.

Josh was a typical young man with the same love for athletics as the rest of his family. He was very bright; however, he was challenged with reading English. His tutor, a dear friend of mine from high school, Victoria Olividoti, introduced me to Josh and his parents to help him with his reading challenges.

Again, as is the norm, Josh was limited in the words he could read from our pre-test. He avoided much eye contact with me and was somewhat reserved. When I asked him about his reading, he responded that he wanted to be able to read as well or better than the other students in his class at school and currently he wasn't able to do that. Josh was an impressive young man who stepped up to the challenge and overpowered and slew some significant dragons that day.

At the end of our 2 1/2-hour instruction, Josh confidently read all the words from our GED list and, according to Victoria, returned home with much more confidence and stronger interest in reading. I was pleased to have his uncle and mom there to witness the change in reading fluency and to hear Joshua read 475 words without hesitation. We have observed that overcoming reading challenges enhances life challenges.

It is so important to me, my having been an athlete in high school and not a very good student, to help bring a balance of academic success to those who excel as athletes. From what I have been told, Josh will now go on to become an excellent athlete like his father and now, at the same time, have the opportunity to excel in school.

I am looking forward to hearing more about Josh's achievements.

Chapter 11

The Great Man

"Surround yourself with Greatness, some of it will rub off. Every day, I read something. Form a habit of reading every day!" Bob Proctor

Craig Collins and Bob Proctor at CEOSpace

My intention for traveling to Toronto was to meet with Bob Proctor, the esteemed and well-known motivational speaker featured in the movie *The Secret*. After several negotiations with his skilled assistant, I was invited to his home to share with him our Universal Reading Method.

When I arrived at Bob Proctor's home, I was seated in the beautifully furnished formal living room. On the coffee table I opened a large book about Steven Spielberg and as I looked at the different pictures from his life, I remembered that Spielberg is dyslexic and only recently let his grandson interview him and tell the world.

While waiting for Bob Proctor, I looked down at my watch and saw that the date was November 28th and remembered that I could be celebrating both the anniversary of my mother's birth, and in the States it was Thanksgiving Day. For me, it was enough I was sitting in Bob Proctor's living room, someone I respected and admired for the many achievements he had accomplished in his life, making preparation to share with him our Universal Reading Method video.

It's my observation that everyone experiences a positive change after I introduce them to our Universal Reading Method. I was curious as to what would take place for Bob. My best wish was that he would express an interest in endorsing us after he watched our video because of his personal experience.

The plan was for me to spend a couple of hours with Bob . . . and he extended our time to 4 ½ hours. The way that I share our Universal Reading Method with folks is to have them participate as if they were a student so they will know what it feels like, either for their own benefit or to recommend that others experience it.

So, Bob agreed for me to teach him our Universal Reading Method as a student . . . and, obviously, he was one of my best students. As usual, I introduced him to some aspects of reading he had never considered before. Most people, like Bob, read because they have memorized the words they know. So, when they can have immediate access to words they have never seen in print before it is quite impressive.

After viewing out Universal Reading Method video for the first hour I think he really got into it and I heard him laugh when he successfully read our somewhat challenging 24-letter, 9-syllable fictitious word.

At the 15-minute break, we walked outside together into the new fallen snow and ice-covered wonderland, where we had to both be careful not to slip and fall. Wearing his signature blue long-sleeved shirt and dark trousers framed by his long black cashmere overcoat, Bob turned right to walk along his street, with a reflective look on his face, already consolidating the instruction.

I turned left, allowing him time to be alone in his process. I was on an adventure to discover the beautiful homes in his neighborhood.

Bob was an incredible speaker and orator with an enormous vocabulary. When he read aloud our 475 multi-syllable words, he did so in the same fashion as he speaks before hundreds of people in audiences all over the world, this time using the seven concepts he learned from our Universal Reading Method.

When Bob Proctor commits to give you his time, he does so 100%, with complete attention to everything you share with him. Having not spent much time with him before this, I understood why he was revered by so many people and has so many followers.

It was a delight to spend the afternoon with Bob. His parting words were: "When you have your Universal Reading Method up and running on the Internet please get back in touch with me."

We are pleased to announce that time is now!

Chapter 12

From Stroke Victim To Recovery

Back in California it was pouring down rain the day that I met Lewis Simms. He and his wife arrived chauffeured by his stepdaughter, Valerie, from the airport via Ohio.

As I walked out to the car to greet him, he nodded with a slurred hello, gave me a quick handshake, and, looking determined, walked past me, to a short flight of stairs that lead to the apartment where he was to learn our Universal Reading Method.

I noticed Lewis was limping and supporting the right side of his body with a polio crutch. Climbing the stairs was very difficult for him, so I stood behind him to catch him if he fell. I admired his determination as he, without my physical intervention, reached the top step and entered the apartment.

His wife explained that Lewis had had two strokes and a heart attack two years earlier that left him paralyzed on the right side and had affected his speech. They had come specifically for Lewis to learn to read and then they'd drive up to Fresno to attend Lewis's high school reunion.

Valerie shared with me, "It was very sad that Lewis could not read because he had a college degree in Electrical Engineering and before his stroke he loved to read. Lewis and my mother had only been married a short 3 or 4 years before he was afflicted."

I had spoken with Lewis's wife Mary on the phone prior to

arranging for him to have a session with us. I had no idea he was paralyzed on the right side of his body and slurred his speech. This was going to be a huge challenge for us.

I had gotten both Mary and Lewis' s permission to video his session and to invite Dr. Barry Schwartz, a neuroscientist, to observe and take notes. Dr. Schwartz was there to observe the neurological affect our instruction might have on Lewis.

With his wife, his stepdaughter, and Dr. Schwartz settled in the living room around the corner with a view from the back of our session, and Richard Crawford, my good friend and film producer setting up the lighting and cameras to record our experience, I conducted a brief interview with Lewis.

I asked him just a few questions to determine if he was conscious as to time and space, questions I had learned when I worked on an acute psychiatric unit while I was studying to be a clinical psychiatric social worker:

"What is your name?"

With slurred and muffled speech, he said, "Lewis," without saying his last name.

"How old are you?"

"I am 63 years old!"

From the front room I heard his wife, with a nervous laugh, shout out, "Lewis, you know you are 69 years old!"

With resolve and eyes cast down, Lewis, very quietly, and shaking his head in disdain, mumbled, "69 . . . I am 69!"

Then, since I knew he was traveling the next day to his high school reunion and had been born in and lived for many years in

Fresno, I asked, "Lewis, where were you born?"

As he stared at me, no words came from his mouth, he just stared blankly at me and it was clear he could not tell me.

My next question was, "Are you attending an event in Fresno?" Again, he looked down. At this point I stopped asking him questions for fear my questions were overwhelming him and might cause him to shut down during the instruction, which I wanted to avoid.

A bit concerned, I asked Dr. Schwartz if I could have a moment with him. As we opened the sliding door to a small balcony, a cold wind rushed over us, cooling my heated face, and as the rain came down hard, I looked out into it and said, "Barry, I am afraid to teach Lewis. He is just too injured."

Barry listened to my fears and, after contemplating for a brief time, said, "I want you to try to teach him, just break it down and make it as easy for him as possible. Don't ask him to repeat a line of information, make it one sound at a time."

As, I returned to the dining room table, where Richard had the microphones ready for Lewis and me to attach to our shirts, I made my decision on how to provide him our instruction. I kept thinking about "planting all of the seven concepts of our Universal Reading Method on his brain very slowly," as if his brain were a hard drive on a computer, without expectation.

The lighting was focused on the table, and Richard's assistant was ready with the extra camera on a tripod. Richard, having overheard Lewis' s response to my questions, as always, was very supportive with compassion and understanding for the cards I had been dealt.

So, after a few firm "I will Thy will be done statements" to myself, I sat down at the table with Lewis.

I gave my nod to Richard and commenced to teach Lewis Simms our Universal Reading Method by asking Lewis to read some small words from our pre-test. The words on the first line were: see, red, milk, was . . . Second line: then, jar, letter, city . . .. Lewis, a degreed electrical engineer, was unable to read any of these words, including the word 'red'. The instructions for the pre-test suggest that we stop the pre-test when our student has missed more than three words. I discontinued asking him to read any more words and asked him no more questions.

The next hour was filled with my saying one sound at a time and Lewis successfully repeating what I was saying each time. I was careful to not require him to pronounce more than one letter sound, as prescribed by Dr. Schwartz. Lewis repeated what I said without affect and in a monotone.

As we proceeded with the short vowel and consonant blends something happened. Dr. Schwartz was standing up in the living room and Richard was trying to get my attention, both pointing to their mouth. Lewis was no longer slurring his words. He was pronouncing every sound correctly! I was so focused on staying on track that I had not noticed. Apparently, this was huge for Dr. Schwartz, from a neurological standpoint. The injury to his brain had caused the slurring and in the first twenty minutes he had stopped slurring.

With more optimism and a clear vision, I continued to slowly and methodically teach Lewis the first six concepts. After about an hour and a half we came to the end of our sixth concept where our students are instructed on how to read a 24-letter, 9-syllable fictitious word.

Again, I took him slowly through each of the nine syllables of our long multi-syllable word and he was able to follow along with my instruction and read the word, with great effort. This was in huge contrast to his inability to read the smaller words during our pre-test.

After reading the word, Lewis was soaked in perspiration but there was a new focus in his eyes. He was more confident, and his interactions were more animated and interactive.

It was time for a break, a 15-minute break for him to rest and consolidate what he had just accomplished. Our students usually take a brief walk outside and get some fresh air but remembering Lewis's struggle when walking up the stairs, I invited him to sit outside on the patio and just relax.

To my surprise, Lewis announced: "No, I would like to take a walk with my step-daughter!" I stood up from the table, to move out of his way, and to our amazement Lewis stood up, did not put all of his weight on his crutch, and instead just used it to steady himself. He offered his arm to his stepdaughter. As they walked out the front door, I instructed both of them to return in 15 minutes.

After the door closed, Mary said quietly, "This is amazing. Lewis hates to take a walk. It is usually just too difficult for him!"

Dr. Schwartz was impressed with what he had observed, especially the improvement in his speech, the change in his confidence, and his walking without relying on his crutch to support his body.

It was, at that moment, when discussing Lewis with Dr.

Schwartz, I realized, for the first time, the Universal Reading Method may be actually having a profound impact on the rewiring of our learner's brains.

Our Universal Reading Method doesn't only teach reading. Lewis was showing some of the same behavioral changes, at the same sequence, our other students had expressed who had not had a stroke. I felt thankful that Dr. Schwartz was with us to make his own observations.

I was excited to continue our instruction and I began to look for Lewis to return from his walk. After 20 minutes, he walked in the door smiling with his stepdaughter. Valarie apologetically explained Lewis had opted to walk down and back up a flight of stairs to check out some ducks who were playing in the ponds created by our rain. Amazing, just amazing.

After welcoming Lewis back, I asked him to return to the table and, on his own, study some papers that had the instruction we had covered before his walk. As I handed the papers to him for his review, he looked me straight in the eyes for the first time, listening intently to my brief instruction. Lewis sat there for the full 15 minutes looking at each concept and talking quietly to himself, repeating the sounds I had taught him.

After the time allotted, we were ready to continue with teaching him the exceptional sounds . . . however, Richard was having some technical difficulties and needed to go to his car for a fresh battery for one of the mics. Lewis had to wait until he returned.

While waiting for the new battery, Lewis picked up a *Time Magazine*, opened it to an article that had no pictures or graphs, and sat in his chair calmly and stared at the page for about 10 minutes. He never took his eyes off the page. I did not ask him any questions. Lewis was very focused on the words on the page. I have no idea if he was reading but he was definitely not distracted or looking around the room. During my time teaching Lewis, he certainly qualified as my most surprising student, ever.

With both mics working, I began saying each exceptional sound, starting with "*ck*" like in the word "*black*" . . . of which each time he repeated exactly what I said. Once again, his repeating was in a monotone.

As we progressed to the third column of exceptional sounds, I said "*ion*" like in the word "*million*" and Lewis said, without expression, "*ion*" and then "*million*" and then he said, "*MILLION!* I KNOW THE WORD MILLION!" with recognition and excitement.

As he went back to the proceeding exceptional sounds and read them again, without any coaching from me, "*black, walked* and *played, believe, good, food,*" etc. When Lewis returned to the word "million," he said "*million*" then went forward with the words I had not taught him and said, "*vision, nation, jealous, serious, sing, song,* and thirteen more words, 42 words in all, correctly and with confidence. I have no words to describe the joy I witnessed on his face as he read those words. It was as if a light had gone on for him . . . and it had.

After his exciting discovery, Lewis was exhausted. I decided to stop at that point and require no more from him, leaving him with his full consciousness that he had succeeded. Lewis had read our 24-letter, 9- syllable fictitious word and now was correctly pronouncing the 42 words associated with the exceptional sounds, which required applying all seven of the concepts we had just taught him. Dr. Schwartz concurred with my decision and was more than satisfied with the transformation he had witnessed.

I heard from Mary after they returned from the reunion. She told me that Lewis became the navigator for their drive to Fresno. Once there, he knew what streets to take to arrive at the school. In addition, he recognized many of his schoolmates from his growing-up years and spoke with them.

Lewis is one happy reader and is continuing to improve his ability to function in his world. Mary shared with me that Lewis is currently enjoying a word identification game where a whole page is filled with letters and he identifies the words they make from top to bottom and left to right and that sometimes they overlap.

Would you like to meet Lewis Simms and view his progress? https://www.youtube.com/watch?v=7JHuV73WUaA

As a result of Dr. Schwartz witnessing the phenomenal changes in Lewis Simms and following our success with other students, he has brought our Universal Reading Method to the attention of the UCSD neuroscience lab where they will activate brain scans on several students before and after the instruction from our teaching the URM video. We are excited about the value of the results and hope to see them published in a professional journal in a neuroscience study.

To learn more about the hypothesis Dr. Barry Schwartz has designed for the study, please turn to the next chapter.

Chapter 13

Lisa, a Female Stroke Victim Gets Back Her Life

DATE: January 29th, 2017

NAME: Lisa , Stroke victim last Thanksgiving, November, 2016

Married to an engineer, eleven children (7 adopted), and 6 grand children. Attending UCF seeking a Bachelors degree major in psychology and triple minor in sociology, cognitive science, and crime law & deviance combined with certification in behavioral forensics which will be completed Dec 2017.

AGE: 42

Observed Changes in Sleep from Husband:

Husband shares: Lisa is getting five hours and longer of uninterrupted sleep during the first week after the URM. She reports that this is the first time she has been able to sleep since puberty. In addition, she is able to take a 30 minute power-nap before our kids return home from school. Something she never was able to before her strokes!

Observations from Lisa:

So, the first day after the URM, I was able to focus on what I was reading without having to reread things 5 or 8 times. Moreover, I found myself over the next few days experiencing less severe and less frequent headaches. Over the next few weeks, I found I was reading for pleasure again.

I am able to wake up in the morning and exercise again, participate in yoga, and take longer walks for my health. I am, finally, able to focus on me. Essentially, I have been given my life back after learning the Universal Reading Method.

I must tell you that after my stroke in November, 2016, I thought life was over and continued to move forward but without hope. I am fairly intelligent, thirst for knowledge from diverse sources, and live a blessed life. My stroke robbed that from me, for a time. I was depressed, contemplated walking away from my family, and suffered horrendous low self-esteem.

Today, I know my place, I know my purpose, I am fully seated in my mind, at this time. I am currently experiencing a forward movement feeling toward my goals. Before I had thought this was no longer an option.

The URM didn't teach me to read on a basic level. It opened up a door to places in my mind and brain that allowed me to heal, bypass things that may have been broken during the stroke, and gave me new options for learning and digesting information. What I can tell you the Universal Reading Method did for me, most, was provide me with the ability to read, focus, pronounce, and reshape my vocabulary. The stroke caused me to stutter, for the first time; forget words that I had known all of my life, forget names of people I know, and overall, robbed me of the higher language functions that I had enjoyed my whole life.

Today, I still have a few memory problems, but I no longer have any speech issues. I no longer have a language overload that causes me to have an overwhelming urge to cry. I now feel confident in who I am and, in my ability, to conquer the world and, at the same time accept and enjoy the process, as I, again, receive my successes.

I have learned that I must embrace the, "suck" (the bad stuff) that happens in order to accept the next phase of my life.

I lived the stroke. I am still recovering from the stroke, but more important, after learning the Universal Reading Method, I have embraced my recovery from the stroke and reached out to my therapist, Rie Anderson.

Chapter 14

Barry Schwartz Phd, (Neuroscience) Unveils The Magic

Video Interview of Dr. Barry Schwartz:
https://youtu.be/HiqQnI_n7wo

> *"Nothing is more creative . . . or destructive than a brilliant mind with a purpose.* Dan Brown, *Inferno*

Dr. Barry Schwartz

So, what just took place in the brains of both of those Stroke Victims when we provided them with our seven concepts and they were able to read?

Below are observations from Dr. Barry Schwartz

The Universal Reading Method has:

- <u>Hierarchical organization</u>

Teaches a nested hierarchy of rules and exceptions; this is parallel to our development of concepts, as we see in the genus and differentia of dictionary definitions.

- <u>Manageable number of rules</u>

Learner's working memory is respected because there are seven major rules – i.e., within the venerable magical number: $7 +/- 2$.

- <u>"Learning by doing"</u>

Exploration of rules is done with constant feedback, both from one's own voice and the pacing of the instructor/video. Several modalities - motor, auditory, visual, and touch - are involved.

- Serves to stimulate previously under-utilized pathways between Parieto-Temporal and Occipito-Temporal regions and feeds more input to the Broca's area.

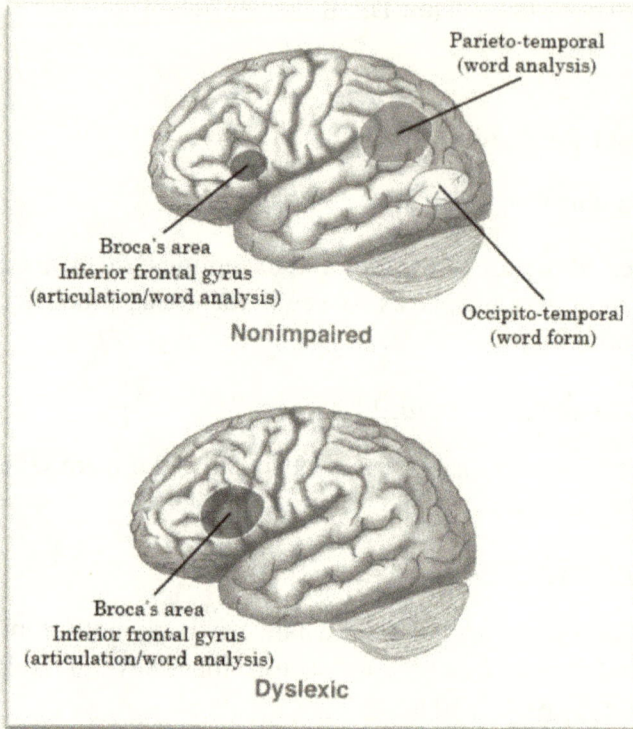

Brain Comparison

• Is an enjoyable process, not drudgery.

• An "insight" form of learning is taking place. The pattern of creative discovery has this feature, a rapt attention, followed by a sudden reorganization of perspective.

• Students do not forget how to read after being exposed to this method; it becomes forever planted in their brain, regardless of how many years they could not read.

• The 1/2-hour break between the two teaching sessions allows memory to be consolidated - while deliberate oral and listening attention is given a rest.

• Reaches a large cross-section of students who have a history of difficulties reading English.

- Responds favorably to pre- and post-brain scanning research because of the shortness of time it is taught. We will be able to pre-scan, pretest, teach the method, post-test, and post-scan all in the same day without any confounded interruption or additional distractive stimuli.

- The ability to be taught on an online format to students, on their computers, at home. The delivery is straightforward and does not rely, beyond what is possible to duplicate with technology, on a live, human instructor.

I have personally interviewed students after the method and observed several students learning to read from the Universal Reading Method, inclusive of a stroke victim with severe right brain dysfunction who showed impressive improvement after one 3-hour instruction session with Mr. Collins.

I am very enthusiastically developing a neurological/brain imaging study involving the Universal Reading Method at the University of California at San Diego, to investigate, document, scan, and report the neurological and learning changes that I have observed taking place in the brain with reading-challenged subjects after a 1 1/2 to 2 1/2 hour instruction session. This instruction session would be inclusive of a 30-minute oral and verbal rest period, allowing for consolidation and independent review of the materials.

~Barry Schwartz PhD (Neuroscience)

As I traveled across the US, Canada, the UK, and Hawaii, I was proud to share the following *Letter of Introduction*, from Dr. Schwartz.

This letter from Dr. Schwartz opened a lot of doors for us while I traveled around the country on our Literacy Tour and invites you to join us in transforming someone you know into a reader. We are now a part of a MEG, brain imaging scientific study at UCSD co-chaired by Dr. Schwartz.

LETTER OF INTRODUCTION FROM DR. SCHWARTZ

TO WHOM IT MAY CONCERN:

I am Dr. Barry Schwartz, PhD (neuroscience). I am currently involved in a brain imaging Research Study in collaboration with the University of California at San Diego to determine long-lasting changes in the brain's functional pathways that occur once a student receives the 2 ½ hour teaching provided by the Universal Reading Method. I have worked with colleagues in the past on research studies that measure such brain rewiring resulting from external injury. This time we have the opportunity to chart the course of changes in function which are both constructive and rapid.

The Universal Reading Method was invented by Doug Collins and further developed by Craig Collins and I have observed it transform challenged readers from limited reading ability, including a 69-year-old multiple-stroke victim, to levels that exceed the requirement for reading of a post-high school student in 2 ½ hours.

It is because of the remarkably short period of time it is taught and the dramatic results it produces that I have decided to conduct a brain-imaging research project to document the changes I have observed and then publish our findings.

It is with confidence that I introduce you to Craig Collins, the CEO of the Universal Reading Method, Corp., who is currently traveling across the United States, into Canada and the UK, Hawaii, teaching students from all ages with reading-challenge diagnosis and who speak with an accent and/or when English is their second language.

I invite you to give Craig Collins an opportunity to teach your students, and request that you will support his efforts to reach many more students with the Universal Reading Method. His goal is to continue speaking to college and university departments, service clubs, schools, and receive opportunities to transform as many students in the world as possible. Please refer him to students you may know who have been diagnosed with reading disabilities. Enjoy as you witness their transformation.

I am personally excited about the upcoming launch of the Online Universal Reading Method because of the impact this skill-set will have on the numbers of challenged students and how it will transform in the world.

Please feel free to contact me if you have any questions regarding the Universal Reading Method and/or our current research.

Sincerely,

Barry Schwartz, PhD.

Chapter 15

Asperger Syndrome: A New Freedom To Choose A New Life

"It takes a village to raise a child. It takes a child with autism to raise the consciousness of the village." Coach Elaine Hall

One of my first students with Asperger's Syndrome was a young man, 16 years old. His name was Harris. I believe that several of my students were undiagnosed and very possibly had Asperger's Syndrome or some form of autism.

When Harris was a baby, his mother put him in his playpen at night after he had a vaccination at their doctor's office. Each morning she would go to him to welcome him to his day and he would be standing up, smiling and always ready for her to pick him up. But, this day, he was still asleep at the bottom of the play pen. When she woke him up, he was really groggy and did not seem to recognize her. It was the saddest day of her life. After speaking with several doctors and specialists, her son was diagnosed with Asperger's Syndrome.

I met Harris in his mother's car. Harris was sitting in the backseat, behind her, while she was driving. So, it was easy for me to see him and talk with him from the passenger seat. During our drive to their home, she recounted her story about when Harris was diagnosed with Asperger's Syndrome and spoke openly, in front of him, about it and his being autistic. Harris seemed comfortable with her communication with me.

When we arrived at their home, after a quick snack, I sat down with Harris in the living room and asked him to read from one of the 4th-grade books he had that were sitting on a table.

Harris exclaimed that he could read from these books. So, I picked one up and asked him to read it to me. As he opened it and began to read, I realized he wasn't reading it but, instead, telling me a story about what he thought the book was like. As I put my finger on each word, in attempt to discover what his reading level was, it was obvious that he could not read any of the words. Once I discovered his reading challenges, we left the books in the living room and I invited him to come into the kitchen with me and sit at the table.

I sincerely did not want to embarrass him, so I did not require that he attempt to read from our pre-test. I knew that the words on our pre-test were even more difficult than the ones in the books he had been unable to read. It was important to me not to emphasize his being a non-reader.

After we were situated at the kitchen table, I began to teach him our Universal Reading Method. This was before the time when we had created any of our videos, so it gave me an opportunity to teach Harris at the same speed I had taught Lewis, our student who had had two strokes and a heart attack.

As with Lewis, Harris was able to understand me and was easily learning each concept of our Universal Reading Method. At no time did he hesitate to pronounce out loud any of the sounds that we teach.

To my surprise, Harris began scratching the back of his head, pulled at his hair, and then rubbed his eyes. He announced to me with fear in his eyes that he was having an "autistic meltdown." I was aware that our students begin to touch their head in the middle of the 4th concept, but never before has anyone expressed that they were having a panic attack. I was quite amazed because there was no build-up to his expression of impending emotional doom. In addition, Harris was doing amazingly well, and it was obvious he was easily learning everything I had taught him so far.

So, I announced to him that I did not know anything about autistic meltdowns nor much about autism. I explained to him that I only know about teaching reading. Then I told him I was very impressed with his progress and that he was progressing amazingly well.

I suggested that he run upstairs to the bathroom, splash some water on his face, talk to his mom, if he needed to, and, if possible, please return as soon as he could, since he was doing so and I did not want his success to be interrupted.

Again, he tried to tell me more about his meltdown . . . and as he spoke, I pointed to the staircase and upstairs to the bathroom.

While he was gone, I prayed until I heard the water stop running and the bathroom door open. After a short pause I heard his footsteps on the stairs, and he re-emerged and sat down next to me and we resumed his instruction. At the end of the sixth concept he successfully read our fictitious 29-letter, 7-syllable word, with no more talk about his "meltdown."

During his 15-minute break, he went into the garage and pulled out a very large tricycle and rode it in a circle around their circular driveway, waving and smiling at me each time he passed by.

After the break, he returned to the kitchen table. I handed him the pages I had been using to teach him and asked him to review them, out loud, like he had repeated them with me. With little indifference, Harris studied and read aloud all the concepts, one through six, he had been taught earlier.

After his 15-minute review time, we returned to the instruction and he easily learned all the exceptional sounds. Immediately on completion of our Universal Reading Method, I handed him five sheets of paper printed with 475 multi-syllable words on them.

It is important to share with you, at this point, I had no idea how Harris would do when reading the words. I was still a little cautious because of his unexpected talk about an autistic meltdown. So, I, after taking a breath, asked him to begin reading them to me.

As he came to the first word, 'evergreen', he looked at it for a quick second and then, speaking under his breath with a question mark at the end, said "evergreen?" From that point on, speaking articulately and clearly, Harris read all 475 of the post-high school multi-syllable words. And, at the end, he smiled big and offered me a "high-five."

At that moment, without us hearing her, his mother entered the kitchen from the stairwell and asked, "How are you boys doing?" Harris immediately slid out from his side of the kitchen table and walked towards his mom, handing her all five pages of words, and announced: "I did great! I read all of these words."

Having experienced Harris telling me he could read from the 4th-grade books earlier with enthusiasm when he couldn't, I understood his mom when she smiled without much emotion, looking at the multiples of long words on the sheet, and said, "That's wonderful, Harris!"

As she spoke, Harris recognized "that look" on her face and the sound in her voice and said, "No, Mom, I really can!" He then walked towards her, placing his left hand on her left shoulder, of which she, surprisingly, looked at to assure herself it was Harris's hand, as he reached around with his right arm and hand, over her right shoulder, and pointing to the words, again read all of the 475 words, speaking into her right ear. When she showed a shocked emotion, he comforted her and told her, "It is OK, Mom. I can read now!"

After his mother returned upstairs, Harris invited me to see his tree fort. As he took out his keys and unlocked all four of the locks on the door, I could see that he was very proud to show me his fort. Inside were all his special treasures he had collected: an orange traffic cone, some tools, and assorted knickknacks he had found in the street and around his yard. He even had me climb a ladder to the second floor and look inside a large wooden chest. I had no idea this was an important moment for him.

Once we exited his fort and returned to the kitchen, his mother came down in preparation
to drive me back to my host family's home, and asked us, "What have you guys been doing?"

I told her, casually, "Harris just showed me the inside of his fort and all of the treasures he has collected."

I saw a surprised look on her face as she said, "Harris showed you the inside of his fort? No one has ever seen the inside of his fort! After his father built it for him, he put the locks on it and hasn't even let his father look inside or any of his brothers. That is really unusual!"

Four years after I taught Harris our Universal Reading Method, I heard from a friend of the family who works with Harris's mom:

Harris has graduated from high school; he has a girlfriend whom he took to the prom; he has been accepted to college and wants to study to become a Christian minister; and has definitely matured into being a more independent young man.

Teaching Harris was another realization we were transforming the brain of our students in more ways than teaching them to read.

Chapter 16

Jenny, With The Light Brown Hair...

In San Diego, a good friend of mine, who was aware I was teaching students to read no matter what their reading challenges were, introduced me to her friend Kathy who had a 27-year-old daughter living at home who had been diagnosed, like Harris, with Asperger's Syndrome.

I so admired her friend, because her daughter Jenny did not share an identity in her family as someone with a negative label. Her mother just loved her and had never labeled her.

Jenny could read a few small words and no words with more than 5 to 6 letters, and absolutely no multi-syllable words when I pre-tested her.

In addition, I was told that when she took a walk Jenny would often lose her concentration and get lost . . . even for short distances.

While Jenny was watching and learning from our video, I purposely left her alone and I spoke with her mother at the nearby pool where they were vacationing. I wanted to teach a student with our video without my involvement, just like she'd be learning if her mother had purchased our Online Universal Reading Method and there was not an instructor involved.

I returned after the first hour to accompany Jenny during her consolidation break and walk. With a big smile on her face, Jenny said, "No, I can do this by myself!" and, with shoulders back and confidence, walked out the door.

I prayed for her while she was gone.

She returned in exactly 15 minutes . . . without getting lost. She did not need me, and I was thrilled.

After she returned, she studied the method from the review papers I provided her, and then, again, following the instruction on our video, she returned to the video and mastered the exceptional sounds.

When she was finished, in two hours and ten minutes, I listened to her, confidently and with lots of volume in her voice, read 475 post-high school words. Next, she read from a book she brought with her and then explained to me the content.

This young person touched my heart.

A few months later I received an email from her mother:

"My daughter is reading all of the time and at dinner she likes to tell me all about what she has just read and discusses many topics. She has decided to move into independent living and has much more confidence in herself since she learned your Universal Reading Method."

Thank you, Jenny, for having the courage to show up for your future. And, thank you, Kathy, for taking the chance we were right in our assumption that your daughter would learn to read.

Our experience with transforming the reading skill-set for students who have been diagnosed with severe reading and, oftentimes, developmental disabilities is growing rapidly. Overcoming word challenges makes life challenges easier . . . with a remarkable increase of self-confidence when our students learn our

Universal Reading Method.

Another quick story is about Dane, a 10 year old, diagnosed with Asperger syndrome, look-alike Harry Potter, also diagnosed with dyslexia.

Dane, arrived to his video instruction, with a great attitude, dressed like Harry Potter, carrying the first Harry Potter book, The Sorcerer's Stone under his arm. He even had on the Harry glasses and his sideburns were cut appropriately.

So, it was easy for me to tell him, "I have some magic for you today that you will be able to use to read, any word you wish to!" With bright eyes and enthusiasm he took a more intense look at me and nodded his head in the affirmative.

As I tested Dane, to determine if he could read a few words, he proved to not read any of the 40 words I provided him from a WRAT3 pre-test. Although, he enthusiastically claimed before I asked him to read the words, "Yes, I can read words!"

So, smiling, I secretly took a breath and lead him over to my lap top and explained to him, I would not be able to answer any of his questions once he began. He assured me, "I have no questions, let's get started!"

As I sat behind Dane, while he was watching the screen and repeating the sounds that I, as the teacher on the screen, directed him, I became aware, that he was doing exactly what I directed him to do and was not skipping or missing anything.

In addition, I noticed that his posture and focus on the screen had improved and that when I asked him to take a walk, he made full eye contact with me and assured me, with confidence, he could walk around on the sidewalks around my home, and successfully return in 15 minutes. I shared my watch with him and Dane returned in 15 minutes.

After using the bathroom, he returned to participate in the Review and succeeded in adapting to some of the additions I had developed for our students when pronouncing the consonant/vowel sounds.

After learning the exceptional sounds, which required him to use and read 40 words, words like nation, vision, and million.....jealous and serious....and, walked and played, I remembered that Dane could not read the word "red" before we started! So, I was somewhat prepared for what happened next!

Sitting between his grandmother and myself, on a couch, I handed Dane 11 pages, 475 words that I gathered from the GED word list for persons taking a test to enter college and asked him to use the seven concepts that he learned from the computer instruction to read them.

I am not sure if you are guessing correctly, but as his grandmother and I shared a few tears, Dane proceeded to read ALL of the words on the pages, to the point when he was challenged with a few more difficult words, reminding him of the concepts required to read that word, I let him proceed forward, so as not to interfere with his enthusiasm and joy.

This was truly a Harry Potter moment, filled with magic for Dane. But it doesn't stop here! Remember Harry Potter's, The Sorcerers Stone that Dane had brought with him? When I asked Dane if he would like to read "that book" he had brought with him, he exclaimed, "It will work with that too!" and ran off the bring it back to the the couch!   "Dane, pick out a chapter you want to read from the Table of Contents!" I said, and then turned away.   First he hesitated, an old habit, and then opened his book, found the list of chapters and immediately, using his finger to scroll down, picked out a chapter!   He seemed to show some recognition of the chapter he chose and when I inquired, he told me, "I remember this from one of the Harry Potter movies, I saw...... a couple of months ago!"

As I watched listened to Dane read from the chapter he had chosen, aloud, I saw his excitement, enthusiasm and his ability to understand.... comprehend, what he was reading bringing him incredible joy, to the point I could not get him to stop reading from the pages. Not wanting to take him away from his fun, I, after several more pages, placed my hand on the page to interrupt and asked, "What is going on for you?"

"I don't want to stop! This is better than the movie! Can I read more?"

Dane, when he returned home read all of the other Harry Potter books and now that he has returned home has continued to be a good reader and enjoy reading!

Chapter 17

Tomas, Experimenting With Bi-Polar And PTSD

".... 'bipolar disorder' is partly caused by an underlying problem with specific brain circuits and the balance of brain chemicals called neurotransmitters."

Teaching students to read in Palo Alto, California was amazing. I was hosted by a woman, whom I had met at CEOSpace International.

CEOSpace is an international business organization to which I belong where I received my introduction to becoming a successful entrepreneur. I met many other people like myself with an "idea and a dream" but no formal education on how to become a successful developer of an idea into a monetized business. I recommend CEOSpace to anyone who is interested in learning more about entrepreneurship and has an idea they want to turn into a product.

Upon my arrival in Palo Alto I took a few days off to relax and regroup, just swimming and wandering around this very quaint town on my bicycle. On the third day, I started networking and looking for students to teach. Each morning I went to the corner market for a cup of coffee and soon became friends with the owner and his brother. Both of them introduced me to potential students.

My first student, Tomas, was a very fascinating man who could read, but he wished to have an experience that would contribute to the neurotransmitters and the organization of his brain.

Tomas had fallen off of a bridge and hit his head several years earlier. He also took medicine for a bi-polar disorder. He had complained of having difficulty sleeping and felt he might have ADHD. Of significance, Tomas is incredibly brilliant and for many years he had been part of a "Think Tank" at Stanford University near Palo Alto.

During my travels I had begun to see a pattern with our students. Each of our students transformed into a reader, which in and of itself is amazing, but something else was happening. I wanted to explore it more thoroughly while in Palo Alto. I was observing other positive changes taking place with our students when they had learned to read.

Initially, when I observed the learners my brother was teaching, I noticed that they shifted the way they were sitting and touched the back of their head after they had received the first half hour of instruction. As they were learning for about 20 minutes, I observed both feet become more firmly planted on the ground and their spine becoming more erect, sitting up straight. Then, they leaned forward towards the instructor or, if learning from the video, towards the screen. Then, I began observing that when the students left for their break they had more eye contact with me. They were more interactive and more expressive with their hands. In some ways, they appeared to be changing their personality, much more assertive.

A year earlier, prior to meeting Tomas, we had taught a student with Asperger's Syndrome to read in Minnesota. After being taught the Universal Reading Method he read at an extremely accelerated rate and showed significant changes in his affect.

When I asked Dr. Schwartz, the neuroscientist, about my observations he referred to "plasticity" and "activating dormant parts of the brain."

The goal of sharing the Universal Reading Method with Tomas was not to teach him to read. His experiencing our instruction, for all intents and purposes, was to help bring him "peace of mind" and to see if we could change the way he was feeling with more opportunity for sleep. The gift of teaching Tomas was in observing someone who had a different agenda for experiencing our reading method. I was looking forward to sharing our instruction experience with Dr. Schwartz. Tomas and I set up an appointment for the next day, a Saturday.

Tomas met me at the corner market where we had first been introduced. We walked the four blocks to his condo. Once there I set up my computer on his dining room table.

Tomas was a reserved man who focused intensely on the instruction he was receiving. I tested him and determined that he was an excellent reader. His session then began as I turned on our Universal Reading Method video.

In the beginning, Tomas spoke very quietly and in a monotone. As he advanced into reading and pronouncing sounds from the list of vowel and consonant sounds, I could hear his diction improve. He then moved closer to the computer screen, speaking louder and with a higher level of emotion and affect.

As Tomas got up to take his 15-minute walk outside, he gave me a great big smile, something I had not seen him do since I had met him two days prior. Grinning as he started out the door, he made an observation while holding the back of his head with both hands.

"I feel a tingling at the back of my head."

When he returned, Tomas conscientiously reviewed aloud for 15 minutes all the materials that I had provided for him. He then turned the video back on to learn the exceptional sounds. After repeating all the exceptional sounds, Thomas immediately read all of the 475 words on our list.

Instead of being a test, reading the words solidifies the seven concepts in the brain. Thomas glanced up after reading the words on the list and gave me another big smile.

"Would you like to hear me play the piano?" he asked to my surprise.

He then took me to his grand piano and proceeded to play several classical pieces for me. His demeanor had changed from serious and distancing to engaging and entertaining. As he played, he kept pace with the music by rocking his head.

I asked him if he played his piano often. He shook his head. "Not for some time!"

There seemed to be a certain calmness and joy flowing through him as his fingers adeptly and with great expertise entertained me. It was delightful.

After the concert, I was most interested in seeing if there would be any changes in his sleep pattern over the next few days.

When I saw Tomas over the next couple of days, he reported to me and the owner of the corner market that he had been able to sleep through the night for the first time in a long while. He reported that he felt more clear and happier than he had for a long time. It was during one of our post-meetings that Thomas shared with me that he had often felt anxious and that for the past days he had not felt any anxiety.

For several days before I took the train south to San Diego, whenever I saw Tomas on the street he would smile and wave at me. He would always give me the Thumbs Up sign to let me know that he was still feeling good from our instruction.

Before I left Palo Alto, about a week later, Tomas invited me to attend a piano concert he was performing at a local church. I told him that I was sorry, but I could not attend. As he was walking away, he responded with a smile, "Too bad. It is going to be fun!"

A year later, during a phone call with Tomas, he explained to me:

"The most profound impact my learning the Universal Reading Method had on me was in accessing my memory of past events in my life, going all the way back to my childhood.

"After falling off the bridge, I only had flashbacks of events in my past, and now I have the whole memory of them. My clarity about my past and the improved efficiency of my memory without the distraction I had before makes it much easier for me to function and has improved my confidence."

There are no scientific conclusions for my observations, but the obvious positive changes in affect and self-confidence provide a fertile field for thought and future exploration with brain imaging research.

Chapter 18

You Mean I Am Not Really Dumb And Stupid?

"There is nothing wrong with my brain?"
I said, "No."
"I am not dumb and stupid?"
"No!" I said, with compassion for how this young man
must have suffered for the last ten years

As I pedaled my bicycle from the home of my sponsor in Palo Alto, the bright sunny day filled my heart with a smile. I was just so filled with joy and I absolutely loved the quaint little town I was enjoying as the warm breeze made havoc with my hair. I felt absolutely centered and grounded from my mile swim prior to climbing onto my bike. It was one of those "grail castle" kind of days and I was definitely asking why I was experiencing it on that morning.

While dropping in for a coffee at the corner market owned by a delightful Mid-Eastern man, I met a 16-year-old young man and his mother who owned the local barber shop a couple of doors away. She shared with concern in her eyes, "My son's teachers are suggesting that he be held back this year at school because he is very behind in his reading." She turned away for a second with emotion and then turned back and said, "Do you think you can help him?" I told her I would love to, and we set a time for the next day in the afternoon to meet at the corner market for us to walk to a nearby park for instruction.

The mother and her son Julien showed up at the market as

planned and he and I walked to the park around the corner. Julien was a tall, likeable, athletic kid.

While I was setting up the computer on a redwood picnic table under a big tree in the beautiful park, Julien watched me intently before we began. With some fear in his eyes and in a soft voice, almost a whisper, still standing, as if he just might run away at that very moment, he looked me in the eyes and whispered:

"I have something to tell you. I am really slow . . . I mean, uh, really slow. I have, uh, some real difficulty when I try to read, especially aloud in class. There may be something wrong with my brain! My teachers want me to be held back a grade this year. . .so I probably won't be able to learn this very well today!"

With sincere compassion and admiration for his sharing, I responded, "That is very interesting, because my brother Doug, the guy who invented our Universal Reading Method, thought he was retarded when he was young and people just weren't telling him because they did not want to hurt his feelings! Possibly he has created something you will understand. I think he would relate to how you feel and, I believe, you are one of the kids he designed this for. He didn't want anyone to go through life feeling the way you just told me you feel."

When I asked him to read words from our pre-test, it was clear that he was able to read at approximately a 4th-grade reading level . . . small words only and no interest nor ability to even try to read words that were multi-syllable or had more than five letters.

So, I set him up with our Universal Reading Method video on my computer and invited him to sit down on the bench. It was a slightly warm, beautiful sunny day in Palo Alto and a perfectly peaceful setting for our instruction to take place.

"I am the instructor in this video so please do everything I ask you to do. It is important that you speak out loud and can hear yourself repeating the sounds that you are being taught. Will you do that?"

He nodded, "Yes, I promise!"

I walked over to the middle of the grass in the park and laid on a large towel I had brought with me taking in the warm rays of the morning sun while I observed from afar our student and listened to him speaking out loud and repeating from our Universal Reading Method.

After about 50 minutes, I observed Julien close the screen to my computer, knowing I was watching, and took off for a 15-minute walk, as the computer program instructed him to do. While he was gone, I placed our review sheets on top of the closed computer for him to study when he returned. I had to admit, not knowing how Julien was feeling since he walked the opposite direction from me, I was praying that he'd return to finish the instruction.

Exactly 15 minutes later, I spied Julien walking around the corner. There was a certain lightness to his walk, his shoulders less rounded. When he saw me, he acknowledged me with a big smile.

As he approached, I reached over and picked up the four review sheets and handed them to him. "Be sure to speak out loud during your review." He nodded affirmatively and went immediately to the review papers.

It is at this time in our instruction, when my students return from their brief walk, I begin to see positive changes in their affect, and Julien was no exception. He looked less afraid and made eye contact with me for a longer period of time.

After he reviewed for 15 minutes, I returned and turned back on the computer for him and directed him to learn the exceptional sounds. After about 20 minutes, he looked up and closed the computer. He was done.

I walked over to the table and handed him five pages with 475 multi-syllable words that were from the GED. He looked at the first word: *evergreen*, pronounced it correctly and then proceeded to read all the words on all five of the next pages as I sat with him at the table.

He was silent for a time and then, looking me straight in the eyes, said, "There is nothing wrong with my brain?"

I said, "No."

"I am not dumb and stupid?"

"No, you just read 475 college-level, multi-syllable words, didn't you?" I asked.

"Yes, I just didn't know they looked like that before but when I heard myself say them, I knew them . . . and had heard them before. And, most of them, I know what they mean!" He smiled. "I don't think the other students in my class can do that."

Standing up abruptly and with an assertive attitude, Julien said, "Let's go show my mom. She is going to be so happy!"

Neither of us could feel the sidewalk under our feet as we walked-skipped excitedly towards where his mom was cutting hair at her shop.

As we walked into her shop, his mom said, "How did it go? Are you already done?"

"Yes." Handing her the pages with the 4- to 5-syllable words he said to her, "Can you read these words?"

His mom took the sheet of words, looked over at them for a few seconds, then, after a brief hesitation and realization, responded, "Most of them!" without reading them aloud.

"Well, I can read all of them!" Julian exclaimed proudly, removing the sheet from her hands, and he commenced to read to her all of the words on the sheet: "Appointment, addictive, adaptable, leather, diminish, accomplish, accident, constructed, displacement . . ."

After he finished reading, Julien's mom grabbed the sheets from his hands. We followed her out the door, walked quickly down to the corner market, and found her friend who had introduced us. He was sitting on a stool behind the counter looking at his computer. With an amusing and challenging look on her face, she quickly placed the list of words on the counter in front of him and inquired, "Can you read these words?"

After the shop owner had looked at the pages, he smiled and said, "Most of them!"

She retorted, with a proud grin, "My son can read all of them!"

It was a happy moment for everyone, especially for my 16-year-old student.

Julien lives in a town right next to Stanford University and just south of Berkeley and San Francisco State. The odds of his attending college had just greatly increased.

The next day I was awakened by the birds singing as the sun filled my bedroom. I rolled out of bed and pulled on my bathing suit. As I swam my morning mile, I found myself smiling as I thought with anticipation about my next student at a nearby convalescent hospital later that day.

Chapter 19

Our Experience With Alzheimer's Syndrome

"Our study suggests that exercising your brain by taking part in reading books and magazines is important for brain health in old age." Robert S. Wilson, Rush University Medical Center in Chicago

Two days later, my host in Palo Alto invited me to visit with someone who lived in a convalescent hospital whom she had decided to visit with once a week. The woman she was visiting was 94 years old and had been diagnosed as having Alzheimer's Syndrome.

I am going to change her name, out of respect for her, and so I can tell you my whole experience with her. So, I have chosen my mother's name, Avis, because I couldn't help but think of my mom when I spent time with this delightful person.

When I first met Avis, she was dressed and sitting in a chair speaking my host in Palo Alto. As I listened to her speak, I immediately fell in deep "like" with her and began to imagine and see her as she might have been when she was much younger and active in her life as a mother and wife.

While the three of us sat on overstuffed couches and chairs in the sitting room of the convalescent home, for two hours I told her about my travels teaching our Universal Reading Method. She shared with me she had not read for several years and wished to begin again and thought our method might help her to begin reading again.

Just before we were leaving, I arranged to return the next day to talk with her again and set up a time when I would teach her our Universal Reading Method. When we bid farewell, Avis graciously with her very kind and warm smile told me:

"I am looking forward to talking with you tomorrow. Come at 10:00 a.m., after I finish my breakfast."

As I walked out, since I had been told she was in the early stages of Alzheimer's, I was a bit confused, since our conversation had been so fluid, with an exchange of feeling and emotion. She seemed so "normal."

The next morning I got up, had some light breakfast, rode my bike to the corner market for some coffee, talked to the "boys" on the corner, and checked my watch several times, so as to be on time to meet with Avis at the convalescent home.

I locked my bike to a bike rack in front of the convalescent hospital, enjoying the beautiful weather, as I prepared to enter the facility.

As I rode up the elevator to the 4th floor I thought about my conversation with Avis the day before. She was the age my mother would have been if she were alive and I felt a kind of nurturing anticipation and pleasure in seeing her again.

Before I walked into the room, I peeked in and there was my new friend, sitting up in bed still having her breakfast. The curtains were open and there was sunshine flowing through the windows, illuminating her. Her eyes were bright with life, as I sat down next to her bed and said, "Good morning, Avis. How is your breakfast?"

Avis looked at me with a polite smile and with a welcoming voice, said, "I am so sorry, but I don't think I know you!"

It was then I remembered what I had been told, so with my best smile I could muster, I said, "I am Craig Collins and we met yesterday!"

Avis smiled and said matter-of-factly, "I don't think we have met before, but you seem like a nice man."

I was immediately reminded of the movie and the book, *The Notebook*, a story about a man whose wife had Alzheimer's Syndrome and only remembered him on occasion.

Recovering from my surprise (that I was sure I was prepared for) I reintroduced myself and we spoke for about an hour and as we did, she relaxed and spoke with me as she had the day before, still not remembering me.

After a time, I again told her about our Universal Reading Method and she announced to me, "I have not read for several years and would love to start reading again. I am a good reader, but I need just a little review to get going again!" So, we set the date for tomorrow and the time for 9:30 a.m.

While I was preparing to leave, Avis said, "I will tell the nurse to have me up, dressed, my hair combed—oh, how my hair must look today—and fed so we can begin immediately after you arrive. You say, 2 ½ hours, do you? Well, that will be perfect. You are a nice man and I will look forward to seeing you tomorrow!"

Amused, I again was reminded of my mom and then several scenes from *The Notebook*.

That night I rode my bike into downtown Palo Alto and listened to some impressive music from a Reggae singer/guitarist on the street. As I sat near the music, I noticed that just up the street was The Tin

Pot Creamery, a gourmet ice cream salon. So, with people standing outside, without hesitation and in all decadence, I ordered a banana split.

While waiting in line I spoke to folks who worked for Google and were attending college at nearby Stanford. The evening weather was warm and balmy. I could smell the fragrance of summer in the evening air and it filled me with peaceful and happy thoughts.

The next day, as I woke up, I heard the birds singing and enjoyed the early morning sun shining through my bedroom window. I rolled out of bed and pulled on my bathing suit. Walking down the steps to the pool at the condo where I was staying, I thought about my very dear student for that day. Swimming my morning mile, I found myself smiling as I thought with anticipation about what magic might happen with her at the nearby convalescent home today.

As I traveled across the United States teaching students, it became interesting for me to observe the changes in the brain I was witnessing. So, you can imagine my excitement at having an opportunity to provide our Universal Reading Method to someone who was diagnosed with Alzheimer's Syndrome and who had not recognized me the next day after what felt like a fairly long and significant encounter. What changes would Avis experience and would they be obvious? Would she be able to read after we finished the instruction?

And even more pressing at the moment, would she remember me? What would I do if she didn't? No matter what, I wanted to make sure I had the opportunity to teach her.

I again remembered my feelings after reading *The Notebook*, and how it must have felt for the husband to have not been recognized day after day and then recognized only on occasion. So, I was prepared, or so I thought I was, for the gifts of my day.

As I rode up the elevator to the 4th floor and walked down the hall, I approached Avis's room. I peered in, a bit timidly, and observed that the curtains were still drawn. As I tiptoed into the room, I saw her breakfast on a small table with wheels and found her in a deep sleep, with her mouth open, lying on her back, slightly snoring.

My heart fell a bit because I was so excited to teach her with my many questions as to how this might impact her and others with Alzheimer's Syndrome. As I began to leave, not wanting to bother her, I noticed that she was stirring, first the left eye opened, then the right eye, and then she saw me. She asked, "Can I have some water?" So, I poured her some water into one of those powder blue plastic glasses with the red plastic straw in it and handed it to her.

As she held the cup, she looked up at me and said, "Are you new? I do not know you!"

At that moment, the attendants came in and took over.

"Your visit is on the board, but I did not see it. I am so sorry. Let me get her up and dress her. Can you sit in the waiting room? I will come get you in a few minutes," stated the very sweet, small Filipino nurse.

"Of course!" I responded, and walked, a little challenged, down the hall to where Avis and I had sat and had our first conversation.

As I sat down, I saw other patients I had spoken with on that day, and as if God knew I needed a bit of a lift, two of them remembered me and said, "Hello." One of them even asked me if I was here to teach Avis our reading method. His remembering our conversation helped give me more confidence.

At that moment, the attendant found me and announced, "Avis is ready for you now!"

As I walked towards Avis's room and entered, I fully realized and accepted that I was going to have to start over with her. She did not remember me, and I was going to have to come up with something. So, when I entered the room, she smiled at me, her hair combed, make-up on, sitting up dressed in a blue silk blouse, and still in her bed.

I, again, introduced myself. "I am Craig. I have been invited to talk to you and I do something very special!"

"And what is that?" she inquired.

"I teach folks to read!"

"How delightful!" I heard her say.

"Do you read much anymore?" I inquired.

"No, I had a book started when I moved here, but haven't picked it up for some time."

"Well, our reading method helps to 'jump start' people who haven't read for a while. Would you like for me to share our reading method with you? The woman I was supposed to teach forgot and isn't really available right now for me to teach."

"Sure, I would like to see what you have to share. Besides, you might say, I have the time!" she kidded politely, with a wink.

I began by saying, "I apologize for giving you this short test, but I am curious how much you may have forgotten about words since you moved here."

Avis responded, "Oh, I think I might have forgotten more than you would have guessed! I tried reading my Bible recently and couldn't locate one of my favorite verses."

During the pre-test, Avis could read many of the small words and only some of the longer words. I stopped testing her so as not to embarrass her after she missed more than three of the words and began to look confused. I did not want her to get stuck in the identity of not being able to read,

For the next fifteen minutes, I introduced her to our Universal Reading Method and like with our stroke victim in San Diego, I modified the method and taught her one sound at a time, instead of whole lines of information at one time.

After teaching her for about 20 minutes, Avis looked up, and with bright eyes and recognition said, "Hello, how are you, Craig? Where is your friend?"

As I continued to provide her our instruction, I watched her eyes become brighter and her affect more engaged. For the first time, she was remembering me from three days before.

Over the course of our 2 ½ hours I observed Avis beginning slowly and then building, mastering each concept and, at the end of our instruction, successfully and easily reading our fictitious 29-letter, 9-syllable word. She was very amused and articulate when she read the exceptions . . . nodding her head knowingly as she articulated each one of them. It was as if when she read the exceptional sounds she was recognizing something she already knew.

After successfully reading several pages of the multi-syllable words, she leaned towards me, reaching out with her hand to touch mine, and inquired, "Craig, could I read to you, instead of continuing reading these words, a special verse from my Bible? It is in the drawer, as are my glasses."

"Of course, I would love to hear you read from the Bible!" I said with a bit of curiosity and feeling pleased and surprised. It is more significant to me that she read from a book or the Bible than from the list of words. Reading the words definitely set the stage for her to read sentences.

Again, as with the other students I have taught, Avis was looking different, in more contact and with purpose . . . as I handed her the Bible and glasses. Without hesitation, Avis knew what Bible verse she was looking for; knew what it said and why she had chosen it, thumbed through her Bible, found it by Book and number, and read it with emphasis and eloquence—her reading glasses on the end of her nose—looking quite like the teacher she once was.

I was blown away. Her demeanor was impressively interactive, and she was expressing from a very conscious state of mind.

American King James Version (AKJV)

JAMES 1:17

"Every good gift and every perfect gift is from above, coming down from the Father of the Heavenly lights, who does not change like shifting shadows."

After she finished reading to me from her Bible, she told me there was another book in the drawer that she started some time ago.

As I sat in the chair across from her, she announced, "I have 18 grandchildren," and told me about parts of her life with her husband and about a time when they used to sit on the steps outside of opera houses and listen to the singing.

And amazing of all amazing things, Avis asked me, "Would you like me to sing you my favorite opera song?" Then she sang me a song from an opera she liked and told me, "I learned this song before we had money and could afford to buy a ticket and sit inside."

Knowing nothing about Alzheimer's Syndrome, but interested in if she was now able to have memory of current events in her life, like recalling the conversation we had three days ago, I began to explore. She remembered the name of my host and the day she looked forward to her visit. We talked about those visits and what they spoke about.

Then Avis spoke of some of the budding relationships involving the aides and nurses who worked in the hospital. She added that she didn't like the food at the convalescent hospital, especially the hot dogs a few days ago. As I stood to leave, she remembered some personal things I had told her about my life.

When I left Avis, after sharing our Universal Reading Method with her, I felt like I had witnessed a miracle . . . and was anxious to return the next day to see what, if anything, she remembered about our time together that day.

Up early the next day, bright and bushy tailed, I returned to check in on Avis despite my worst fear that she may not remember me or still be able to read.

I was remembering a movie I once loved when I was in high school. It was a movie starring Cliff Robertson, *Charly*, based on a book called *Flowers for Algernon*. In the movie, Charly is a man who is educationally challenged, who was injected with a magic potion that appeared to reverse, for a certain amount of time, his limited ability to mature and learn things. Algernon was the name of the mouse who was part of the experiment and who also had been injected. In the movie, Algernon died, and Charly returned to his childlike personality.

I braced myself and held my breath as I rode the elevator to the 4th floor and walked into Avis's room unannounced. She was sitting on top of her bed talking with her daughter and my friend, who was sitting in a chair next to her.

When I walked in, Avis looked up and, recognizing me, announced to her daughter, "This is the man I told you about. This is Craig, who came to visit with me. He taught me his reading method!"

In this instance, Algernon lived, and Avis maintained her ability to read.

While my friend was talking with Avis, her daughter took my arm and ushered me down the hall. "What did you do with my mom yesterday? She is so animated today and talking about so many things . . . and with more enthusiasm than I have seen for quite some while! She even remembered all of her 18 grandchildren's names and even what she gave them for Christmas three years ago!"

I explained, "My brother has developed a reading method and I have begun observing changes in our students' brains that goes beyond teaching them to read. So, I was curious if we could have a positive impact on folks with Alzheimer's."

For the next couple of days, I visited with Avis and each time she remembered me and greeted me with a welcoming smile and lots of stories.

Finally, it was time to return to San Diego. While sitting on the passenger side of my friend Nathan's truck, I reflected on the three amazing learners I had taught in Palo Alto: Julien, the 16 year old; Tomas, the Think Tank man; and, Avis. While releasing a deep breath, I smiled and thought how amazing it would be if our Universal Reading Method could create a similar scenario as it had with Avis with other folks with Alzheimer's Syndrome! I couldn't wait to share all of this with our team, especially Dr. Barry Schwartz, our neuroscience advisor.

Again, it is very important to me not to invite and possibly disappoint people who have or know someone who has Alzheimer's Syndrome and create a hope that they can be brought back to a conscious interactive level by learning our Universal Reading Method. The experiences we had with our students are factual and their significance is limited based on being an observation and an interpretation of those observations.

We are interested in further exploring the possibilities and I have a friend who owns an extended care facility with a focus on gerontology. So, there is a possibility of our receiving additional students who have been diagnosed with Alzheimer's Syndrome and attempt to set up a scientific study to continue to explore if they have a brain imaging response and change in mental functioning after we expose them to our Universal Reading Method.

Chapter 20

Can You Teach A Speed Reader To Read?

"As funny as it seems, I feel like I have accessed new parts of myself after learning your Universal Reading Method and thus feel more in balance and immediately had a lasting sense of inner peace and a feeling of increased self-esteem."

Gary, lifelong speed reader

Often, I am asked, "What happens when people who *can* read learn the Universal Reading Method?"

Here is a story about my teaching a man and his wife while sitting on a bench outside of a library in Encinitas, California, on a beautiful sunny summer day. Both Gary and his wife Jeanne were excellent readers. They became interested in our reading method after I shared with them that it was very possible that we may be causing the brain to rewire in some way, as well as teaching someone to read. I had this conversation with Gary very close to after we had taught Lewis Simms, our stroke victim.

Please enjoy this writing Gary sent me, about a week later, after I, personally, taught his wife and him our Universal Reading Method:

"I am Gary, a business entrepreneur. I am 55 years old. My wife and I are not your usual students because we did not come to you complaining about our reading ability. Our curiosity was more as a business reference. As such, I believe our experience may be significant regarding how your Universal Reading Method is affecting the brain of your students. For us there was definitely a neurological, psychological and emotional transformation we never

expected from participating in your two- hour instruction process.

Here's a quick overview of what I've experienced over the past two days since you taught me the Universal Reading Method. In the order they occurred to me from Friday through Sunday early eve . . . Since the time I took the Speed Reading course in the 8th grade and was taught to read whole words and blocks of words I have had difficulty speaking with proper articulation. I feel that what has added to this problem that in this class we were told to never move our lips nor open our mouth when we read. After that I always felt a little inhibited reading and speaking out-loud. To combat this, when I came to sounds I did not know, I would speak quickly and slur over them.

After learning your reading method, I can actually feel my mouth moving and hear myself saying the sounds in each word. When I speak, I am speaking slower, with more confidence in clearer and warmer tones that I can feel inside my chest. I feel I have something to say and people can now hear me and will listen to me. It has provided a new inner feeling of confidence for me.

For quite some time I have felt somewhat out of balance with my world. As funny as it seems, I feel like I have accessed new parts of myself after learning your Universal Reading Method and thus feel more in balance and immediately have a lasting sense of inner peace and a feeling of increased self-esteem. I began to feel that way while you were teaching us, and it just kept building and continues to do so during the following days

At first my attention to what you were teaching was not important to me, and then I realized I was learning things I had never learned before about words, and as you spoke, I began to have a sense they may be connected in some ways to unlocking parts of me I have wanted to access for a long time. As my attitude changed my healthy self-esteem actually increased as well.

When I was looking out the window, at home the next morning, I actually could see better. My vision was much more vivid, and everything seemed brighter. You are gonna laugh, but since I was feeling so good when I woke up, I went around the house looking at things I am accustomed to seeing and, asking myself, "Have other parts of me changed, as well?" Guess what, since I was feeling more playful and younger, I looked in the mirror and, possibly, because of the inner smile radiating from me, I actually look younger.

In following with my connection to a younger me, later in the day I enjoyed watching the neighbor kids play with their dogs and while watching them I felt more like a child myself. I just have this smile on my face . . . something that has been gone in my too hectic life for so long I can barely remember when I have felt this way before. And all of this, I feel, because of learning to identify and repeat all of the sounds in words in a specific order and in seven concepts. My new awareness definitely feels like an inner response from my participation with you.

At first, because of my experience of being graded when I was 13 and told that I was an excellent reader, and because of the speed of which I could read and the high level of comprehension I had, I did not think I was going to get anything personally for me out of listening to you teach it, other than a better idea of what you are doing. Boy was I surprised!

Like when we were outdoors sitting on the bench in the park and you were teaching me and my wife . . . when the train whistle blew and then the siren from an ambulance followed it . . . I just took a pause for the cause and resumed my train of thought when it was quiet again.

In the past I would have been very distracted and have forgotten everything I was thinking. This same new ability to selective screen outside distraction continued when I arrived home. In general, I feel much more tolerant to changes in my day-to-day life. While writing this I was waiting for a scheduled appointment to show up and he didn't. This would have normally sent me through the roof, but for some reason I felt calm and accepting of it.

Always, I feel a strong need to check in on my computer. For the first time in a year, I did not turn on my computer for two days, did not even feel the need to watch television, required less food, and in general just felt an overall satisfaction with myself.

Once I applied for a job with a company that sold pharmaceuticals to doctors' offices. During the interview I was asked to read a list of medical terminology. Since I had never been exposed to medical words, I could not read the words on the list. If I had not memorized a word, then I had no idea how to read or say it. This new awareness and transformation are somethings I am very excited about.

I find it interesting that although I have been formally trained to be a speed reader, I am no longer trying to read fast. I prefer to hear each sound that is in words and let them resonate within me. I want to hear the words and experience them fully, and then reading them in sentences, take their meaning deeper into a feeling part of me.

There seems to be a lot I missed from speed reading everything I read, although giving me an illusion that my doing so was a statement about my increased intelligence. Now, I realize just how intelligent I really am and how easy it is to access my intelligence.

This is all new to me. Until now I actually did not know the words I read and spoke easily from memorizing thousands of them. It is just more enjoyable to read now, and I am getting so much more from the content! And it definitely feels like many other parts of me have shifted, as well!

I am wondering if anyone else has experienced these significant shifts in consciousness after being taught your reading method. My wife, although not quite as dramatic as I have, has expressed she felt an immediate rush of good feelings about herself, also. The flow of her reading and speaking when I was listening to her also seemed to flow easier.

Thank you very much, Craig, for sharing the valuable Universal Reading Method instruction with Jeanne and me!

Thank you, Gary, for your testimonial. When I meet someone who is inquiring about our Universal Reading Method and they are avid readers, I ask them this question: "Why do you pronounce a vowel long or short? How do you know? Do you have a specific reason?"

They usually tell me they have memorized it and it just sounds right. In addition, they acknowledge there are words that they "don't know" or that they "do know." To know a word is to have memorized it.

When our students have learned the seven concepts to reading from our Universal Reading Method, they know specifically why each of the vowels are long or short; and when they pronounce and read every word that appears on a written page, they do not come to a word they cannot read and they may never had known them before.

Imagine the amount of space that is taken up in the brain storing all of the possible 1,025,110 words in the English language, as of January 1, 2014. What if in the place of all those memorized words you just had to know seven easy concepts? Possibly, there would be more room in your brain to take in more interesting information. Possibly, when you became older your memory would be more easily accessed.

We don't know if this is true or not but hope to find out soon from our brain imaging study at UCSD.

Chapter 21

Does Speaking With An Accent Interfere With Learning To Read?

"There are approximately 25 million adults in the UK who are functionally illiterate."

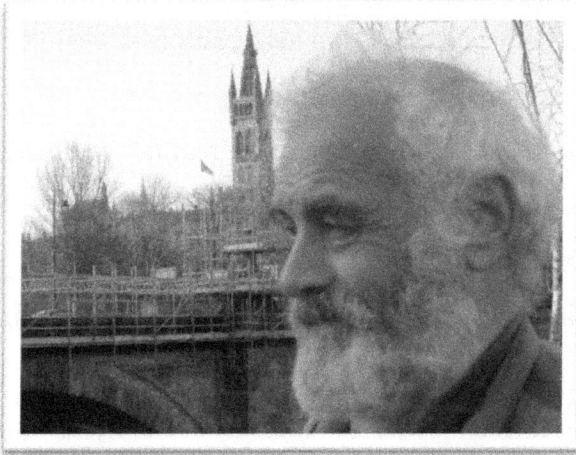

While on a train, traveling toward Watford, England, outside of London, I met a very dear man. He was sitting next to me and we struck up a conversation. He asked me where I was from, and I told with him the United States. He smiled and said he guessed by my clothes and my looking a wee bit confused as to where I was. I told him I was on my way back from London where I visited all the famous places. He shared with me that he had lived in England all of his life and had never traveled very far away from there.

As we talked his trust in me built and he spoke of his grandchildren and the sister he lived with. He actually smelled of lavender soap and that grandfather-kind of shaving cream. Talking to him on the train was really fun for me, and people in the UK were quite easy to talk to.

"I am traveling around the world bringing the gift of reading to anyone who wishes to learn. I do this in 2 ½ hours." We discussed all the places I had been teaching students and the types of students I have taught. "Age is not an issue. Everyone learns to read when I teach them." He had an interest in my passion and asked me questions about the folks I have taught. From his questions, I begin to realize he may have some challenges with reading.

He spoke to me proudly of being a grandfather, and that he was a stone carrier, his hands worn from working many hours. His bright eyes were topped with furry eyebrows, his face full of deep-set lines: laugh lines from incredible joy . . . and the deeper ones from worry and stress. His lips were turned down as he approached me to share a secret. Leaning towards me, eyes darting to the side, he whispered: "I cannot utter one word from the page. I had babies and had to leave my schooling before I learned."

As we stood there near the door of the train car on the underground to Central London, I asked him, "What are your plans for the next three hours?"

For the first time he looked straight at me, our eyes met, and then looking to the right and up and then back to me, he said, with just a tad more volume over the sound of the train clicking on the track, "I have the rest of my day free!"

"You have a fancy to learn to read, do you?" I said, in my best English accent. He studied me closely, like a man considering his fate.

After, what felt like an eternity of being scrutinized, and careful that no one overheard, he exclaimed, "Why not? Let's do it!"

"Jacob," he turned towards me and shook my hand as he announced his name.

"Craig," as I shook his cold, very strong, calloused hand. I was reminded of shaking my grandfather's hand when I was a "wee little man." He was just that kind of rugged "salt-of-the-earth" kind of man.

As it turned out, his sister lived just one exit past mine. "My sister has a computer!" In my backpack I had a copy of our Universal Reading Method video on an exterior hard drive.

So, we both got off the train and he went to a phone booth to call his sister.

On our way towards his sister's flat Jacob announced, "I am 77 years old. My grandchildren are asking me to read to them . . . and I am running out of excuses."

As we walked, as in other parts of London, I was impressed with the lack of clutter on the sidewalks and the care that has been taken with the painting the iron fences and little pots of flowers on the steps of each small flat.

Somewhat distracted in thought as we walked several blocks in silence, I realized my companion had stopped, so I did, too. Placing his hand on his heart, he nodded towards what appeared to be at least a 10-foot door to a three-story flat. The door was painted shiny enamel black.

Up three floors we climbed, both making male bonding humor about when we "used to *run* up these stairs, often on our visit to bring pleasant joy to a lady friend."

Jacob's sister Sarah Ruth smiled a big smile as she opened the door, inviting me into her immaculately clean flat. Ah, the smell of newly brewed tea.

"Milk . . . and one or two?" meaning, did I want one or two lumps of sugar in it.

"One, and yes!" I felt my accent becoming more English by the moment—possibly from a past life—as I shrugged my shoulders without knowing why.

I was taken to a somewhat older PC with head phones attached. I attached my exterior hard drive to his sister's computer, and then placed her computer on the kitchen table. While Jacob took one of the chairs, resting himself a little away from the edge of the table still not quite sure, it occurred to me that he had probably never sat at a computer before. I plugged the chord into a socket under the table. Jacob looked very curiously at the computer.

I gave him a brief introduction and pre-tested him with a list of words I had with me. He was definitely challenged with reading words . . . even small words. I then placed the headphone on him, patted him on the shoulder, and then pushed the button and our Universal Reading Method video came on. After a short while, I heard Jacob following the directions and speaking the sounds he was being instructed to repeat, somewhat muffled at first then louder as the video instructed him to speak louder.

As I sat behind him in meditative silence, Sarah Ruth sat quietly knitting in a chair across the room to my right, smiling knowingly with her softness and gratitude. As I listened to Jacob with all of his stature repeat aloud concept after concept, I noticed his feet were now planted firmly on the wood floor under his chair and he was sitting closer to the computer peering into the screen, listening with the headphone. His hands were no longer covering his face and he appeared to be sitting taller.

After what seemed like a very short and entertaining time for me, listening and watching Jacob confidently transform, with my seat mate Sarah Ruth, Jacob stood up and, like a man with determination, stated: "It said I have to take a short walk, 15 minutes. I will be back. Do you want to come? No, guess I have to do this by myself." So, with a bit of a jig and a slight limp in his walk he rambled down the stairs.

As we sat there, I regarded Sarah Ruth; her face was flushed, and small tears seemed to be staining her newly applied makeup as they run down her cheeks. I asked her, "Are you OK?"

She attempted to brush them off, using her apron corners to do so, then breathed, "Yes. It has been quite some spell since I have seen him this excited about something. I only remember faintly, maybe when we were both with me mum, a time when he jumped down the stairs that quickly."

I nodded with understanding and compassion for her memory and was on notice: It was working again! The changes were already showing!

When Jacob returned, he immediately went to study the review sheets I had placed on the table next to the computer. He was a man on a mission, with his back to us as he started reviewing without regard for anyone else being around. I was careful not to reveal my Cheshire Cat expression, as we again listened to him repeating the sounds. I smiled assuredly at Sarah Ruth.

As Jacob finished the Exceptional Sounds and shut the computer lid, I immediately got up and walked over to him and handed him five pages of multi-syllable words. Jacob started off slowly, with first short "e", *ever*green…then long "e", ever*green*. I reminded him of our concept of knowing when a vowel is long or short and soon the words were flowing off the tip of his tongue.

Then a light seemed to go on, as he trudged confidently through each page, sitting like a soldier at attention. He shouted out the final 4- and 5-syllable words with a definite statement of pride. When he finished, he slowly placed the list of words down on the table, still glancing at a few words on one of the pages, shaking his head in disbelief that he had just read them.

"I never knew those words looked like that!" Jacob remarked. "At first they appeared to be

just a jumble of letters, then I saw the letters were making sounds and I tried the different

sounds for the vowels and then my mouth just said them, and I recognized having heard them before and knew what most of them meant."

As Jacob explained his reading to his sister and me, I looked over at her and saw the small trickling of tears that were quietly making their way to the sweater Sarah Ruth was knitting. She tried to stifle the sound of her joy mixed with tears as she looked proudly at her older brother.

Then Jacob picked up one of his sister's magazines and read aloud from, of all things, a silly, very unmanly article. Laughing, he put his finger down, holding his place, and said, with every effort to be kind, "Women see life somewhat differently, don't they?"

After closing the magazine and placing it on a small table next to where Sarah Ruth was sitting, Jacob looked directly at me. Then he walked his swarthy frame towards me with both arms held open and gave me a strong, manly hug, always with a slap on the back and a hearty grasp. As he stood there holding me at bay, with a big grin and bright eyes, Jacob exclaimed, "Thank you, me friend!"

As I prepared to leave, I left the copy of the review sheets and vocabulary words on the kitchen table for him. We gave each other another big hug, and then as I was going out the door, I said over my shoulder, "Be sure to go to a bookseller and buy yourself a book or two!"

As I stepped into the landing before going down the steps, there was large paper bag with my name on it right in front of me. You guessed it, in the bag was the sweater Sarah Ruth was knitting and two large jars of orange marmalade. Since it was later now, and getting colder outside, I put my new sweater on. It fit perfectly and as I touched it, I found the place where Sarah Ruth's tears fell, and I begin to feel a big lump in my throat.

Thank you to one of my Scholarship Folks for providing this opportunity to Jacob. You all know who you are. We can teach people like Jacob without a charge because of you. We have friends all over the world who support my travels and transformations. They provide scholarships for many of our students. If you are one of our Angels and have sponsored a student with a scholarship, this story was for you.

Chapter 22

Delightful Folks In Scotland

"Maimie just scored high on her standardized reading test. Her results were impressive."

The car ride from Glasgow to the home of my next students, in Strathaven, was very scenic—through the city and out into the country over rambling roads, through hill and dale. The delightful children of my host family in Glasgow loved to tease me because I had never seen sheep before. During this carriage-like ride, I was entertained by many flocks of sheep contained in stone fences and fields. The wind was blowing and, as is common in this part of Scotland, it was raining, off and on.

I had, around my neck, my favorite Scottish lamb's wool scarf and a blue, Scottish fleece-lined coat and fur-lined hat that covered my ears. Because it was raining and sometimes snowing, I was wearing warm boots and wool socks, as well. When traveling, I always was sure to dress warm and comfortably. It was a different type of cold in Scotland than it had been several weeks ago in New York.

As the windshield wipers moved back and forth, I listened to the mother, who was driving the car, share with me the history of the countryside we were passing through. Based on South Lanarkshire history, weaving had been Strathaven's main industry in the 19th and early 20th century but had been replaced by nearby Glasgow because its proximity to the train.

At the same time, I also could feel the eyes of my two new students staring at me from the back seat while I spoke with their mom. Children in Scotland are very well behaved.

I already liked these folks. Amused by my newly learned Scottish heritage, I wondered if, possibly, they were from the Lamont Scottish Clan, my clan on my mother's side, based on my mother's maiden name, 'Lamb'.

I was so amazed to learn I was definitely from Scottish descent and my family clan was that of "detectives" with a reputation for being very kind and "lamb" like! Since I was an Investigative Consultant for some 40+ years and most people would say a "nice" kind of guy, it really seemed to fit me. When I first learned of my clan connection, I bought and wore a little copy of our family crest on my coat.

Upon arriving at their home, I was introduced to the father and being little awkward about my new Scottish accent, I spoke to everyone in California English, which usually makes everyone smile. The house, as are all homes I visited in Scotland, was immaculately clean and very welcoming, with a warm fire in the living room fireplace.

Outside through the window, next to the table I was teaching from, there were leaves, wind, and rain twirling all over the place. Ah, yes, a real winter, something that is very rare for me, because of my being from California. In the kitchen I could smell something cooking and realized that a meal was being prepared for me, the special guest. It felt good to be honored.

While being introduced to their 12-year-old daughter, she announced to me, "I am the president and founder of The Dyslexic Club at our school." I just loved this little girl's energy and her determination to overcome her reading challenges.

First, I set up to teach her mom with our video, so she would be fully aware of what I was going to be sharing with her daughter. Once I had the video running in the kitchen/dining room with the mom, I walked through the doors to the living room, closing them behind me, and met with my student.

I want you to imagine a young 12-year-old girl who was filled with energy and curiosity with absolute focus to every word I expressed. She had been told by her teachers and the people in charge at her school that she was dyslexic and that wasn't good news. Her parents had been told the same in writing and they, having read with her, were aware of her reading challenges, too. Her mom was an art teacher.

The thing I was impressed with, at my first encounter, was that my student was a very confident and bright child, and it was obvious had parents who loved their children very much and had no embarrassment or lack of confidence in their intelligence. There was no shame in this child, only acceptance for who she was as a person.

In addition, I want you to imagine a young girl who was charismatic and who decided, on her own, to establish a club strictly for people who could not read, kids who had been evaluated as being dyslexic. Her club was so popular that everyone in her class wanted to be in it, regardless if they could read or not, so she had to restrict the membership to just those who really could not read! At this sitting, I felt she had decided this was the day she was going to learn to read. I couldn't agree with her more.

So, with no further delay, I pre-tested her by having her read from a list of words. She was able to read many of the smaller words but when it came to the longer and multi-syllable words, she told me, "I do not know those words!" She was such a poised talker, I was surprised just how very hard it was for her to read.

As I personally taught her our Universal Reading Method without a video, I was impressed as she embraced every concept with enthusiasm and receptivity. There was not part of any of our seven concepts she didn't understand and absorb wholeheartedly. At the end of the hour when it came time to read our 24-letter, 9-syllable word, she put her hand up, with her index finger to her lips, to silence me and read our 24-letter, 9-syllable word without my saying one word, without any assistance.

During our session, I had the occasion to speak to her using my newly acquired Scottish accent so as she exited through the kitchen, she, with a big and nonjudgmental smile, commented to her mom, "Mr. Collins also speaks with a Scottish accent. I think he might be a wee bit Scottish . . . but I can't tell where he is from." Then off she went with the dog to the backyard and the magic of the wind and the leaves.

As the daughter was running outside, her mother, who was learning from our Universal Reading Method video, was returning from her 15-minute consolidation walk. While her daughter was outside, I shared with her that her daughter was doing great and that she just read, with ease, our 24-letter, 9-syllable fictitious word. I could tell from the look on her face, the mother wanted to say, "I did too!" but she just nodded and smiled and went back to her review of the pages I had shared with her.

Both of my students were very attentive.

When my young Scottish student returned from outside, removing her coat, wearing a very confident smile, we returned to the living room. I stoked the fire and put on a few more pieces of wood, feeling a "wee" chill in the room. Like her mom, I give her our four review sheets to look over by herself and left her to study alone.

By this time, the mother was halfway through the exceptional sounds in the other room, so I returned to her. I was able to sit with her for 15 minutes, listen to her master them, and then provide her with our list of 475 multi-syllable words. As I was walking through the door to the living room, I heard the mother successfully reading quickly through the words.

In doing so, I laughed because I was obviously multitasking and, to my delight, I was providing a transformation experience for two delightful ladies.

As the 12-year-old daughter—old beyond her years—began to read from our list of 475 multi-syllable words, I could feel my heart beating and felt a big smile forming on my face.

She read all the words on each page with confidence and clarity. It was as if she had been reading for many years. Listening to her touched my heart and watching her smile, getting bigger and bigger with each discovery of another word she comprehended and was now reading, was, as always, my reminder of why I was traveling the world doing this. Thank you, Doug Collins, for your discovery.

At the end, we smiled back and forth at each other. I asked her: "So, what do you think!"

"What do I think?" she retorted, "I think I will have to resign as president of the Dyslexia Club! That is what I think! I can read!"

As we walked back into the kitchen she said to her mother, "It was hard, but I learned it! What's for dinner?"

While enjoying the lasagna dinner with the family, we discussed my returning to teach the father and their other daughter, who was younger. I agreed to return the following week. I loved being invited to share a home-cooked meal with this family. They made me feel so welcomed.

The next week I returned to teach the younger daughter and at the same time taught the father with our video. Both transformed beautifully!

During my session with the younger daughter, I needed to get her attention when she was distracted by the dog outside of the window at the desk where we were sitting. It was very important that she stay focused on what I was teaching her.

I surprised her by saying, in my newly acquired and humorous best Scottish, "You be lookin' out the window, are ya? Do I have to get your mum and have her sit here with ya to help ya keep ya mind on me sounds on the pages?"

Startled, she said, smiling, "No, I won't be needin' her help!" After that she stayed focused and I think was amused by my speaking like a Scot. It was a funny time for both of us.

Again, her reading transformed, and the father let go of his reading challenges and showed much confidence as a result of our teaching. As I rode back to Glasgow in the car, the mother told me how thankful she was for the gift that I shared with her family.

After a couple of months, I received this email from the mom.

"Thank you for all of the hard work and hours you spent with my kids. We really enjoyed your company. Maimie has just scored really high on the standardized reading test. Her results were impressive."

Janie McIntyre

Chapter 23

Scotland Loved The Universal Reading Method

"It was as if a door that had previously been bolted shut sprung open and my son's self-belief returned. At the end, I could hardly speak without welling up in tears. I am so proud of my son."

Elizabeth, the mother of one of my students in Scotland

This was one of my greatest joys and rewards for my efforts during my journey around the world. This writing reflects the repeat experience I had with my students wherever I traveled. I especially like the way she allows you to experience her son.

Dear Craig,

Before the lesson with you, my 12-year-old son Alexander could read words that he knew by sight but was embarrassed, frustrated and intimidated by words that were new and unfamiliar, so much so that he would avoid reading like the plague. This, of course, affected his school work but, more importantly, his confidence and self-esteem.

The day before the Universal Reading Method session he had stated, "No, am not doing it! I'm NOT going!" And he cried, "No, I can't do it! I can't read!"

Knowing the above, you can imagine how emotional and grateful I was and still am, as I watched him transform before my eyes during the lesson. In only 2 ½ hours, his somber face changed to one full of delight and amazement, as he tackled and read words he didn't know, and self-pride was bursting out of him.

It was as if a door that had previously been bolted shut sprung open, and my son's belief in himself returned. At the end I could hardly speak without welling up in tears. I am so proud of my son.

The results:

After we returned home, my son asked me to buy him a book . . . well . . . imagine the swell in my heart. Not only that, he reread the list of multi-syllable words to his dad, then, read a couple of pages from a book and a whole chapter from another.

To their delight, Alexander has even been reading stories to his younger siblings, as well. I can't believe how happy he is and more himself than he has been for a very long time.

Alexander said, "I'm glad that my mum made me go, because now I can read words I don't know and it feels good."

To someone who has difficulty with reading, Alexander says, "I would definitely tell them to do it. It's good!"

Thank you so much, Craig.

Yours in gratitude,

Elizabeth and Alexander

Chapter 24

Hawaii, Once Upon A Time, A World Reading Giant

"My desire to learn; my ear to hear; my eyes to see; my hands to handle, for, from the sole of my foot to the crown of my head I love the palapala (reading and writing)."

As I walked down the steps from my Hawaiian Airlines plane, I immediately smelled the ever-present fragrance of plumeria and enjoyed the warm tropical weather all about me. My body became immediately moist as I unbuttoned one of the buttons on my new Hawaiian shirt and hiked my shorts up on my hips.

I had lived in Hawaii during the 1970s and returning to Oahu brought back many wonderful memories. A friend introduced me to this writing about how reading English came to Hawaii. I had no idea:

"King Liholiho Kamehameha II declared in 1818 that all Hawaiians *must learn to read and write English*. The Hawaiian word for reading and writing is *palapala*.

Not long after the passing of Kamehameha I in 1819, the first Christian missionaries arrived at Kailua, Hawaii on March 30, 1820. Their arrival here became the topic of much discussion as Liholiho, known as Kamehameha II, deliberated with his *ali'i* council for 13 days on a plan allowing the missionaries to stay.

Interestingly, the missionaries promised a printing press and to teach *palapala*, or reading and writing. Because Liholiho had learned the alphabet prior to the missionaries' arrival, he had a notion of the value of a printing press and literacy for his people. A key point in Liholiho's plan required the missionaries to first teach the *ali'i* to read and write. The missionaries agreed to the king's terms and instruction began soon after.

During the first year of instruction, the missionaries struggled to learn 'ōlelo Hawai'i (Hawaiian language) and delivered their lessons in English. After one year of English instruction, four pupils had developed such great skill that they were selected to teach English to fellow Hawaiians, including Liholiho's son Kauikeaouli (Kamehameha III). To reiterate, in one year's time, this group of Hawaiians learned English well enough to teach their peers!

On January 7, 1822, the first eight pages of the *pī'apā* were printed, creating the first Hawaiian alphabet book and reading primer. Contrary to popular belief, it was not the missionaries that created the Hawaiian orthography, but it is more likely that the literate Hawaiians of the time deserve credit for that work.

The first printing of 500 *pī'āpā* copies was quickly devoured and 2,000 more were printed six months later. To keep up with the boom in interest and demand, many Hawaiians needed to move quickly from students to teachers. This movement of learning the *palapala* was thought to be good for all ages.

There are accounts of the rapid acquisition of reading and writing by young Hawaiian children in that time. Their prowess was such that they would be "surpassed by few American pupils of a corresponding age." Even Hawaiians in the latter stages of life learned the *palapala* quickly.

Kakupuoki, a widow, at the tender age of eighty tenaciously

pursued literacy. The missionaries questioned her dedication to learning this new technology and even advised her to give up, but Kakupuoki persevered with the assistance of a female attendant and mastered the *palapala* in two to three years.

Hawaiian historian Samuel Manaiakalani Kamakau explains that this was not uncommon and names three individuals over 80 and 90 years that could read the Bible before the end of 1823: Kekupuohi, Kaeleowaipio, and Kamakau.

By August 30, 1825, only three years after the first printing of the *pī'āpā*, 16,000 copies of spelling books, 4,000 copies of a small scripture tract, and 4,000 copies of a catechism had been printed and distributed. On October 8, 1829, it was reported that 120,000 spelling books were printed in Hawaii. These figures suggest that perhaps 90 percent of the Hawaiian population were in possession of a *pī'āpā* book!

This literacy initiative was continually supported by the *ali'i*. Under Liholiho, ships carrying teachers were not charged harbor fees. During a missionary paper shortage, the government stepped in to cover the difference, buying enough paper to print roughly 13,500 books.

In fact, while Liholiho was on his ill–fated trip to England where he, at age 26, and his wife, the queen, died from measles, the regents reiterated their support by proclaiming that upon the completion of schools, "all the people shall learn the *palapala* (learn to read English)."

During this period, there were approximately 182,000 Hawaiians living throughout 1,103 districts in the archipelago.

Extraordinarily, by 1831, the kingdom government financed all infrastructure costs for the 1,103 school houses and furnished them with teachers.

This legendary rise in literacy climbed from a near-zero literacy rate in 1820 to between 91 to 95 percent by 1834. That's only twelve years from the time the first book was printed!

All of this clearly shows that the *kūpuna* were not afraid of any kind of knowledge or technology, and they excelled and mastered it. Equally important, the Hawaiians enjoyed these successes in their mother tongue, *'ōlelo Hawai'i*.

In one missionary account, a young Hawaiian man shared his thirst for knowledge:

"One young man asked me for a book yesterday, and I inquired of him who his teacher was. He replied, "My desire to learn, my ear to hear, my eye to see, my hands to handle, for, from the sole of my foot to the crown of my head I love the *palapala*."

While ancient Hawaiians evolved into some of the world's greatest explorers, traveling the vast Pacific Ocean and choosing Hawai'i as their home, the historical success of teaching literacy recognizes another achievement of these intelligent, capable people. We can all learn from these tech-savvy Hawaiians and draw from their rich history of creativity, innovation, and adaptation.

Our Literacy Tour to Hawaii transformed many currently challenged learners, opened up many doors, and provided me with much personal insight into our teaching readers online.

If you are a challenged reader, possibly fearful that there is something wrong with you, please let go of that thought and click on

our website: www.universalreadingmethod.com and, like the
Hawaiians, learn to read NOW!

Chapter 25

Riding An Entirely New Wave With A Maui Surfer

"My mother and father have spent thousands of dollars trying to teach me how to read. I have had many teachers. I have even traveled to the mainland. I still can't read!"

As I awoke in the home of my host family in Kihei on the Hawaiian island of Maui, I could feel the heat of the day beginning very early. I was perspiring, already bringing a glisten to my face and arms. It was going to be a warm Maui day.

Running down the stairs and out the door, I hopped on my bike and was off to the Starbucks where I was to meet the mother of my next student. I was smiling with anticipation and excitement because, once again, we were providing a transformation experience for a 16-year-old challenged reader. I felt that familiar confidence and knowing that had accompanied me when I had first taken off around the world to teach challenged readers to read two years earlier.

While awaiting the arrival of my student and his mother at our planned meeting place at the Piilani Village Shopping Center, I had time to reflect on the reading transformations I had witnessed of other 16-year-old students while in the UK, Chicago, New York and Palo Alto.

I smiled, looking forward to witnessing another young man who would, very soon, enter a life that he had always believed would be denied him. Does he think or possibly has he been told that his "brain is broken" or that he was "dumb and stupid" and always would be?

The young man's mother and father discovered our Universal Reading Method while watching my interview on a local television show, "Life on Maui with Steve Freid."
Watch it at Life on Maui with Steven Freid ~ Guest: Craig Collins, Literacy Coach (EP 58)
https://www.youtube.com/watch?v=agJIPoVjeJw

Steven Freid and Craig Collins in Maui

In my initial contact by phone, the mother had told me that they had spent thousands of dollars on tutors and reading programs over their son's young lifetime, in an attempt to teach him to read.

"He just doesn't get it. However, I have always had faith he will. So maybe this is that time."

While reflecting on what was possible for this young man, I looked up and saw two people walking towards me who were recognizing me from my interview.

"Are you Craig?"

I acknowledged that I was as I extended my hand to shake hers. As she and I spoke, I also reached out and shook the hand of my new learner. He made quick eye contact then looked away. I made sure I made eye contact with him as I held onto his hand.

As we walked to her car to drive to their home in Hana, I climbed into the front passenger seat of their SUV as her son got into the back seat, sitting behind his mom. We had a clear view of each other.

While we drove, I told them, "My brother created the Universal Reading Method so that other kids would not have to experience the difficulties with reading that he had while he was growing up." I paused. "My brother had thought he might be 'retarded' because of his difficulty with reading. He thought that people didn't tell him that he was retarded because they didn't want to hurt his feelings," I said as we drove along the beautiful coastline to Hana.

I saw in my peripheral vision, to the back left, that the young man was nodding his head and apparently relating to what I was saying. I explained, "Our Universal Reading Method session will take approximately 2 ½ hours and you will be learning just seven concepts, which makes it easy to learn.

"After approximately one hour, you will be invited to take a brief walk, a break, for 15 minutes. I am looking forward to sharing this with you. I know you will be pleased."

Again, to my back and left, I saw a smile form on his face. He was listening intently. Our "trust relationship" had begun. When I am teaching a student in person, my first contact with them is very important. They can't dislike me. When a student learns online, my identity is not as important.

While we were traveling along the beautiful Pacific Coast near Hana, I saw a whole group of sailboarding surfers riding the Trade Winds and catching waves. Some seemed to be flying off of the waves and into the air. It was a magnificent show and remembered when I was in my twenties riding waves on my Hobie Cat off Diamond Head.

For a while, my new friend in the back spoke of surfing and sailboarding, something on which he was an expert. I welcomed his talking to me and could relate. There is nothing like catching a Hawaii wave, especially on a boat. I was feeling young again, just watching from my scenic passenger seat.

As we arrived at their delightful, very Hana, Maui home, surrounded by palms and tropical fruit trees, we were met by their dog which I bent down to pet and received a welcome lick to my nose. As we all entered the house, we were greeted by a pleasantly cool ocean breeze flowing through the open windows.

After receiving a tall glass of lemon/lime water with ice, I set up my computer and headphones on the dining room table. I was excited about this student learning to read from our video and my not personally providing the instruction.

I learned from this young man that his love of video games and the amount of time he spent playing them was a big advantage for him as he learned to read from his computer. We never lost his attention the whole 2 ½ hours.

"Which do you prefer, your mother in the room and watching

you, or would you like to learn without her present?" I asked.

As is often decided, he opted for his mother to retreat to the upstairs so he could challenge this by himself.

After his mother went upstairs, I reached into my backpack and pulled out a single sheet of words. It was a short reading pre-test that we use with each student prior to their beginning their instruction. The results clarified, for him and for me, his current reading ability.

He read some of the smaller words but when he began to attempt to read the longer and some of the multi-syllable words he announced, "I don't know any of those words." He placed the pre-test on the table and pushed it away, while letting out his breath and looking away from me. I felt compassion for this young man and, at the same time, felt confident he would learn to read.

The more students I teach by video, the more I am impressed with the transformation they receive without my presence adding to the concepts and distracting them. This was another teaching experience that helped me to confirm the results for teaching from our video and online. I kept hearing the words of neuroscientist Barry Schwartz, "Our brains only allow and retain seven to nine concepts at a time."

As I turned on the video and sat in a chair behind him, I listened as he repeated correctly all seven of our concepts. There was no hesitation as he repeated the sounds spoken to him from the video. When he was directed by the video to speak louder, he raised his voice. Impressive.

During the first hour of instruction there were times when he pulled the neck of his t-shirt up over his mouth and shrunk down inside, then emerged again with renewed involvement. Before long, both of his hands began to rub the back of his head while he moved his head back and forth. Often our students rub the back of their head at the same specific time, while reading the second line of the blends in our teaching. Dr. Schwartz says, "This is when there is an increased blood flow to the back part of the brain."

When the time came for his 15-minute break, he jumped up and ran outside with a big smile on his face, looking at me straight in the eyes as he passed by me. He had just successfully read our 24-letter, 9-syllable fictitious word . . . a word longer than he had ever seen before . . . and he was visibly stoked.

While on his break he ran off with exuberant energy with his dog at his heels into the thick pampas grass brush forest that bordered his backyard.

When he returned, he appeared refreshed from a quick shower, his wet hair dripping onto the table. He eagerly grabbed the four sheets of paper with the information he had just learned and began to repeat all the lessons aloud to himself, dismissing me to my chair.

He was clearly a "young man on a mission" as he repeated and reviewed all the information on the four sheets of paper. As I listened, I was impressed with how he continued to improve as the minutes ticked away. He spoke a little muffled at first, but his voice eventually became loud and with full volume as he repeated all of the sounds. He grinned as he reread the long fictitious word that he had first read prior to his walk. This time he read it with even more confidence, loud enough for me to hear.

After his successful 15 minutes of review, my surfer friend with a puffed-up chest, straight spine, and confident nod returned to the video. With volume, he addressed the exceptional sounds with determination. As I listened, I could hear that he was able to pronounce them before the time that the video required. He knew he could read. This day had been a long time coming.

After mastering the exceptions, my 16-year-old Surfer Dude student read from a list of words that included: frequent, celebrate, understand, hospital, circulate, adhesive, appointment, addictive, adaptable, leather, diminish and many more. This was in great contrast to his avoiding most of the pre-test words.

"Okay . . . so now let's do some real reading!" I invited. "Do you have a book you would like to read?"

He ran up to his room and returned with a book that his 12-year-old sister had in her room . . . a sixth-grade book.

After a quick opening and shutting of this book, I said, smiling, "Too easy. You just read all of those long multi-syllable words, so you can read a much harder book now."

I took the book *Hawaii* by James Michener from a nearby wooden desk. As he set aside his sister's book on the table, I saw his eyes focus on the adult book I had in my right hand. His look said, "I can do this," a feeling and look he very likely has when he takes off on a big wave. As I offered him the thick book, he reached out to take it into his hands. For me, this is a key time for a student.

"I have never successfully read from a book before, I mean an adult book like this one, not even a magazine," he hesitantly admitted to me.

"I know. You are going to do just fine!"

He sat down and put his index finger under the first word as he began to read . . . slowly at first . . . then with more confidence . . . then with increased ease. When he was done, I asked him to tell me about what he had just read, and he did so with perfect accuracy.

"The missionaries were not very nice to the Hawaiians!"

"You are a surfer?" I asked. "Do you have any surfing magazines?"

"Sure, I have never read the stories, but I have looked at the pictures," he answered with a big smile.

He ran back upstairs, this time taking two steps at a time. When he returned, a little out of breath, he placed the surfing magazine on the table. He thumbed through it in search of a story and found one with a picture of a shark.

After choosing the shark picture story, he read the first paragraph and then the second one with complete ease. He asked me if he could read the rest of the story. After he had finished, I asked him if he knew what he had read.

"Of course, I do," he answered with cocky confidence. "It is about somebody, like me, who surfs, and there is a shark in the cove."

After he finished reading the story about the shark, I called his mom down and told her what her son has just accomplished. She told me that she had been listening from upstairs and was impressed.

"I am so proud of you!" she warmly said as she gave him a big hug. "I always knew you would be able to read some day and now you can!"

Now that he was done learning to read, he stretched out on the couch.

"My head is buzzing," a proud 16 year old announced as he held his head. "It feels like there is something inside it that is moving!"

He then ran outside and picked me some ripe and delicious native fruit from his trees. When he returned, he looked me straight in the eyes and extended his right hand.

"Thank you, Mr. Collins," he said smiling, as he gave me a firm handshake.

I felt a feeling of pride…another young person's life had changed…and I silently said, "Thank you, Doug!"

The ride back to my drop-off point in Kihei was somewhat quiet with occasional stops along the way for me to take pictures of the sailboarders and look down into the beautiful coves. Both mother and son expressed, "We love living in Hana and in our new home." As I exited their car and bid them farewell, back at the shopping center in Kihei, they both thanked me again.

I was feeling really elated from teaching this young man. As I unlocked the lock on my bicycle and climbed on it to ride back to my friends' home where I was staying, I was thinking to myself, with a smile, "This is always amazing for me. How often does anyone get the opportunity to watch someone miraculously transform their life in just 2 ½ hours?"

Chapter 26

Victor Villasenor Can Read

VIDEO INTERVIEW WITH VICTOR VILLASEÑOR
https://youtu.be/fELI5wC84NQ:

Victor Villaseñor

Victor Villaseñor is a National Best-Selling author of five books. My favorites are: *Rain of Gold; Burro Genius; Snow Goose Global Thanksgiving;* and *Wild Steps of Heaven.* Go to his website to find more: www.victorvillasenor.com.

You might be surprised to learn that he is also on the published list of Famous Authors Who are Dyslexic. Google his name. Victor could not even read his own books aloud at book signings. Instead, to connect to his audience, he became a passionate public speaker.

He has lived in shame all his life, because he could not read. After Victor failed the third grade for the second time, even his best friends beat him up and threw rocks at him.

When he was 20, he finally began to understand how letters were used to spell out words. So, he began to memorize words so he could recognize them on pages. Still, he progressed to only a 7th-grade reading level.

After learning to read online from the Universal Reading Method, at the age of 76, Victor told me:

"For the first time, I was able to read two pages of the book I am currently writing to someone over the phone out-loud! I had never read to anyone before. It was easy and I didn't even have to think about reading it to her! Before it would have taken me an hour. This reading method is Genius!"

During the instruction, Victor cried big tears as he realized that he finally understood how to read. When he talked about it, he cried in memory of all the times he had to "fake it" and was called names, like "Burro" and "Stupid."

His most recent words to me:

"Your reading method could change the very structure of society. It has helped to heal the rage and hate I have felt towards the teachers who embarrassed me when I was unable to learn to read from the instruction they provided me. I have learned on a deeper level that I am "smart, not dumb," something I began to realize years ago as I began writing my books with a 7th-grade reading level.

"You have freed me, opened up my world and provided me a new comfort zone while I am writing my next Best Seller and I want to help you take your Universal Reading Method global."

Chapter 27

A New Beginning in the World for Literacy and You Can Participate...as an Affiliate with Us.

The question that arises at this point in our journey as we seek out and transform the world of challenged readers into confident, competent readers is: How do we reach those 90+ million adults and children in the United States who are functionally illiterate? How do we get in front of those 51% of the students leaving high school, some who have even graduated, who are reading at a 4th-grade level?

The first answer to this question is . . . YOU! We need you to tell everyone you know about our Universal Reading Method.

We have set up an Affiliate Program for you to help spread the word and help us to transform learners into readers.

We are generously paying You 50% for each learner you direct to your own URL. We charge $297.00 to the learner; you receive $148.50. In addition, we are providing you access to our videos and marketing materials to assist you in reaching those in your family and community who are challenged with reading. It is a great opportunity for you to make a significant difference in the lives of many people.

The amazing thing about your participation as an Affiliate is you do not have to teach anyone to read. We have taken care of this for you. Each learner receives instruction by watching a 2 ½ -hour video on the computer.

As you can see from reading this book, we found our learners from people like yourself, the parents of your children's friends and schoolmates, your neighbors, colleagues and friends. From our experience, not being able to read is neither gender nor race related. I have taught Learners to read from a huge diverse population of students from age 6 to 94, both males and females.   One thing they all had in common: Once they could read they expressed themselves with more self-confidence and with a noticeable higher self-esteem, from body language, outward appearance, to the quality of their articulation.

Often the adults I taught were the mothers and fathers of the students I taught. Many were keeping their reading challenge a secret, sometimes from their own families. They believed, based on how they were treated and what they were told when they were young students in school, that there was something wrong with them, often something wrong with their brain.

It does not seem reasonable that 90+ million people in the United States are illiterate, and often cast aside. I was told that in Charleston, South Carolina, they report the number of students that fail fourth grade, mostly non-readers, so they know how many jail cells will be needed when those kids turn 18 years old. What if most of these students were actually bright but just couldn't read?

What if no one has ever really figured out how to teach someone to read and that is why so many learners can't? What if it was easy to learn to read and not hard? What if you, as an Affiliate, could improve the lives of these multi-millions of challenged readers, both adults and children?

Our Universal Reading Method is the only reading method we are aware of that was created and developed by someone who had lived day by day as a non-reader. Using logic, it makes sense that someone like my own brother would be the perfect person to reveal a reading method that would open the doors to reading for someone with the same challenges he had. What he discovered provided him with a whole new way of knowing himself and being in the world. He desired to teach others to read so they would be spared the pain and struggle he endured, and to experience the opportunities and confidence that comes with being able to read.

And for that reason and the incredible success witnessed with our students, we have received the attention of Dr. Barry Schwartz, neuroscientist, and Robyn Perna, Reading Specialist, along with psychologists and educators, and other highly educated, discerning people.

I would like you to hear the words of and introduced you to Robin Perna, a Master Degree, reading specialist from California regarding her personal experience with her niece, learning to read: **https://www.youtube.com/watch?v=VQDMAk2MtM8**

We want to assure you we have done the homework for you. We are looking into the brain and how it works. We are providing you the most cutting edge, easy-to-learn reading instruction for you to offer. As an Affiliate, the Universal Reading Method can be presented to one learner at a time, several, or a whole classroom.

It is not at all necessary to be in the field of teaching reading to be a successful Affiliate. As a matter of fact, as we experimented with educators, tutors, and those who specialized in reading challenges, we learned that *it was almost impossible for someone who had attempted to teach reading for years to restrict themselves to only teach our 7 proven concepts and to not save their students when they were challenged.* We learned it is *when the learners are frustrated and we do not save them,* that a neuropathway opens, and other parts of the brain are accessed that move the student beyond their block.

Many of the students were people who, before, had no hope they would ever read competently, or read at all—students who were autistic (Asperger's Syndrome), brain injured, stroke victims, bi-polar, PTSD, dyslexic, ADD, etc. It did not matter what age, their cultural background, or their gender. They just needed to know the English alphabet.

Our students were not just "kind of" learning to read. Most of our students were showing up not being able to read the smallest of words, and at the end they were reading college level multi-syllable words with ease. And, there was a noticeable increased alertness in their personality.

Our students read and comprehended at a level they nor their teachers believed was possible for them, and once it switched 'On', they never lose it. Their transformed reading function is permanent.

All that is required of you to do is to introduce the learner to the online instruction. Think of your attempting to accelerate the emerging of a butterfly from its cocoon. The transformation does not take place unless you let it transform on its own.

Things you should know about the online instruction when promoting:

1. It will only require the student approximately **2 1/2** hours of time to complete the instruction and experience a reading transformation. The Universal Reading Method has 7 concepts which were developed by a non-reader and therefore very easy to follow for people struggling to read.

2. Our CEO, Craig Collins, traveled across the US; up into Canada; over to Hawaii; and to the UK, successfully transforming a variety of challenged readers into readers from all over the world.

Our Evidenced base is from our own personal efforts and experience teaching students how to read with effective results.

3. We have impressed the scientific community with our success at transforming our learners and have been chosen to participate in a scientific MEG Brain imaging study at the University of California San Diego. The data will show how the brain works and why the Universal Reading Method effectively rewires the brain to be able to read.

4. Our instruction is taught online by our CEO Craig Collins and does not invite or require anyone else to teach it. Our students learn on their own in the privacy of their own home or in a classroom monitored by a teacher.

5. The Universal Reading Method provides an excellent format for individual Learners and Tutors, and Educators in a school setting. The same success is experienced with one student as is experienced with a classroom of students.

The research that has been developed by Dr. Schwartz at UCSD will continue to add to our reputation and further establish us as the most successful and transforming reading method ever introduced to the world.

To become an Affiliate, please go to our website, www.universalreadingmethod.com/affiliate and follow the easy instructions.

Chapter 28

Enjoy The Stories Of Two Professionals

"Together, we can change the world!"

Affiliate Relationships are a way that we are getting the word out and inviting students to learn to read and transform with our Universal Reading Method video, as mentioned in the previous chapter. Two Affiliates, John Soriano and Rie Anderson, report their experience transforming learners.

John Soriano works for a school in Orlando, Florida and after receiving authorization from the school where he works, John taught two students. After each student finished viewing and participating with our Universal Reading Method video, he reported as follows:

John Soriano

"The student I worked with using the Universal Reading Method video moved up 40 Lexile points!

From what I have been reading, one school district mapped out such a movement in her Lexile range to take 3 1/2 months . . . and they stated that was an 'aggressive but attainable goal'. The student I taught accomplished it after just 2 1/2 hours with the URM video.

Another student I worked with today was a 10th-grade girl who couldn't read words like 'urge', 'stalk', and 'clarify'. After the Universal Reading Method, she was able to read through 4- to 5-syllable words with a marked improvement in fluency.

You know, I just realized something. We are the only ones who are actually teaching students to read . . . with your Universal Reading Method. The others are just teaching a student to memorize."
John Soriano to Craig Collins

Another one our Affiliates, Rie Anderson, a therapist, has, for the past several years, provided our Universal Reading Method video because of the significant insights she is experiencing with them after they view it. Some of her clients do not have reading challenges but when they learn the Universal Reading Method, they move forward in their therapy with doors open that did not appear to be able to open before.

When Rie taught an 8-year-old boy to read who was failing in his classes, he became a different young man and amazed his instructors. As you read her report, imagine that he is your son or daughter and that you have heard from the school psychologist and teachers and they *"just don't know what to do with your child because he/she is so far behind."*

Rie Anderson

Aim For Excellence, Inc., Tampa, Florida
Evaluation of Eight-Year-Old Student Before and After The URM
Facilitated By: Rie Anderson, LMHC, M.A., a/b/d Ph.D.
NBCDCH, COFT, CNST, NLP/NS

September 15, 2016

Evaluation and Conclusions:

FSA ELA Reading Practice Test Questions
GRADE 3 – Eight-year-old male

Testing from the School – FSA ELA Reading Practice Test Questions
– Grade 3
Eight-year-old male -

Students must fall into one of five levels with 5 being the highest and 1 being the lowest. (Students at level 1 will be retained). This student tested at level 2 but was told that he might be retained. The above testing indicated that student had a reading deficiency and specific weaknesses were in:

Fluency – the ability to read words smoothly
Comprehension – ability to comprehend what is read

Recommendation by School:

Summer school was recommended as well as student be seen by a physician for treatment of ADD.
The parents felt they were being prepared for their son to be retained in the third grade.

In conversations with the mother I was first told that the school said:
  (1) "He can't read"
  (2) Then "he can't remember what he reads"
  (3) Then "he can't concentrate"

In my evaluation of the test being provided to the student, I determined that the stories were not appropriate for the student and that his disinterest was due to content vs his inability to read or answer the questions. The test was Sub-Standard.

Next, I looked into #3 above:
I tested the student for an ability to concentrate and found him able to focus and concentrate when the subject matter interested him. However, he was easily distracted.

On the Day of Testing:

Student arrived with his mom for the URM appropriately dressed and clean.
Behavior Presenting: High level of agitation with inability to focus.
3rd grade Teacher and/or School Psychologist had given a diagnosis of Attention Deficient Disorder; ADD. I diagnosed him with ADHD and/or ADD

Evaluation of Eight-Year-Old Student Before and After Learning the Universal Reading Method:

Student is presenting signs of Autism with Asperger's Syndrome. In addition, he is high level functioning indicating a sensory processing disorder.

Prior To Learning the Universal Reading Method:

Student does not like school stating it is boring and not interesting. He complained about the beach and family vacations to the beach.

Parents speak English; Maternal Grandmother speaks Spanish and English. Student expressed interest in learning a foreign language. Mom shared that he was good in math. Student utilizes games on his i-tablet. I feel that his math recognition for formulas and solutions and his ability to maintain his focus while participating in games on his iPad provide him with the qualifications I need for him to participate in the instruction provided in the Universal Reading Method video instruction.

As recommended by the School Psychologist, the parents had taken the student to a medical doctor, who gave him a prescription for

Methylphenidate HCL; a generic form of Ritalin.   At the time of the instruction the student was not taking any behavior modification medication.

Post Learning the Universal Reading Method:

During the first three days following being exposed to the video reading instruction, the student exhibited challenging and disinterested behavior in the classroom.

On day 5 after the URM, he was given a classroom science project to complete. Much to the surprise of his teacher, his parents, and, I believe, to the student, he completed the assignment on time, made a presentation in front of the class, and confidently explained to the class during an oral presentation:

(1) what his project assignment had been,
(2) how he went about solving it and
(3) his end results.

The teacher took a photo of him presenting in front of his class and forwarded it to his parents along with a delightful letter about student's performance with the class project. The teacher was quite impressed and expressed she was surprised by the change in the student's personality.

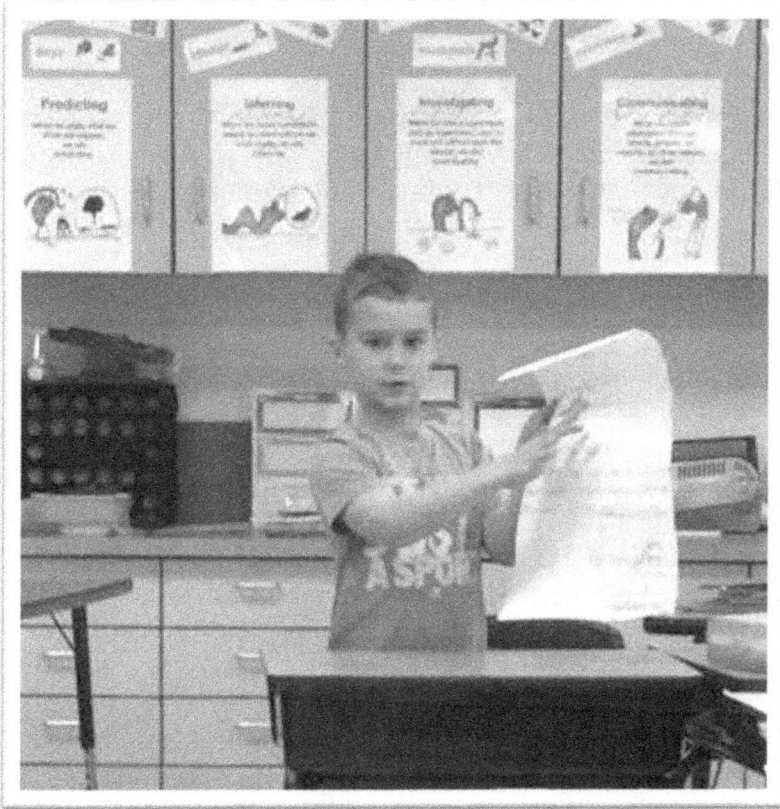

After observing a profound increase in the student's reading, vocabulary and an increased self-confidence, I suggested—and the parents agreed—that the school immediately re-test him using the same evaluation tools they had before. As we expected, because of the changes we had observed, he scored at level 4. The school has positioned him firmly in the Fourth Grade without further consideration for him to be held back.

Non-Academic, Observable, Positive Changes in Personality After URM Instruction:

Student is expressing a higher level of verbal communication with words from a significantly higher-grade level. During the post-instruction exercise, the student successfully read and pronounced 99% of the 475 post-high school multi-syllable words with a high level of fluency.

In addition, his parents are very pleased with his change of attitude about the beach and waves during their recent vacation at the shore. Student participated in boogey-boarding for the first time and spent most of his time in the water, playing in the waves, in huge contrast to his prior feelings and behavior during while at prior beach-oriented vacations.

Results:

It is my professional opinion that the changes that took place during the 2 ½ hour Universal Reading Method instruction for this student brought about the profound increase in his engagement in the classroom and his enjoyment of the water activities during his recent vacation. I am just amazed with his increased reading ability and increased vocabulary. He is no longer a failing, endangered student and I believe he now has the tools to lead a productive and creative life. It is obvious that he now has access to the integration of once dormant parts of his brain.

Rie Anderson, LMHC, M.A., a/b/d Ph.D.
NBCDCH, COFT, CNST, NLP/NS

Another of Rie Anderson's clients who did have challenges with reading and with expressing herself with words was so enthusiastic about her experience that she wrote to me the following testimonial:

"I found Craig Collins's Universal Reading Method an enlightening experience.
My brain felt like letters A to Z from the game Scrabble were in a small jar resting quietly and when the jar was shaken and letters scattered, I knew something very exciting and profound was happening in my brain.
My mentor, Rie Anderson, introduced me to Craig's Universal Reading Method video. It has only been 4 days since my experience. I am aware that words are coming much more easily to express myself and I am understanding in more depth what I am reading.

I am most grateful for this program . . . I recommend teaching the Universal Reading Method to children and adults all over the world!!"

Leah Soderblom
Longboat Key, Florida

If you would like to become an Affiliate, please go to our website:

www.universalreadingmethod.com/affiliate and follow the easy instructions.

Currently, we are pleased to have Affiliates in Australia, London, Scotland, and as well as the United States.

Chapter 29

The Research Future With The Universal Reading Method

One may wonder where the Road to Research began for our Universal Reading Method? For me, it began the first time I watched someone transform from a, dyslexic non-reader into a reader in 2 1/2 hours.

During the first hour of my brother teaching James, an adult mail, he read the words he saw on a law school congratulatory statue during a break from his instruction, at my brother's house. "Sue the Bastards" he announced. Then, aside, speaking confidently, he announced, "Crane God!" while looking at the manufacturers label on a commode" James was kind of tough guy and I believe was delighted these were the first words he read! A light bulb had gone on for James but why and where? Obviously, something had taken place inside of his brain! The only clue he could give to me was it had something to do with his saying the consonant/vowel blends. Sue was his sisters first name so he knew, "Sue", but bastards required a formula and he now had a formula, made up of seven concepts.

So, our journey began with a question, an important question? Why are our learners able to learn to read in just 2 1/2 hours? How is this possible? What is going on in the brain of our Learners? What are we doing that no one else is doing? Not even my brother new the answers to these questions! I certainly didn't, even though I was teaching hundreds of challenged with reading English folks.

Not until we met and listened to Barry Schwartz PhD; (neuroscience) did we even begin to have a clue.   First, I thought it was because my brother, a teacher was very charismatic and it was because he had a special relationship with learners he taught! It is true, Doug's calm communication skills did not distract from the instruction, but there was something more.

After traveling across the Continental US, up into the Western Provinces of Canada, down the East Coast, across the Pond to the UK and back to the East and West Coast, I experienced transforming learners everywhere I went!

From Dr. Schwartz, I learned one of the key factors to our learners transformation, was we were teaching 7, easy to learn and understand, concepts!   The number of concepts was not intentional, but lucky for us, it is exactly the number of concepts a human brain can receive easily and immediately utilize!

This further explained why our successful learners seemed to progress equal or better than when we taught them online, without a live instructor. It became apparent that the presence of a real, live instructor, caused the learner to receive several, very personal concepts, that sometimes, distracted them, as they adjusted to the stimuli by the presence of a human being!   Someone who they have feelings about and who may have feelings about them. It was apparent that seven was the magic number!

My first road to research was to transform lots of learners in many parts of the world and the questions that came up, for us, as I did! Although all of our learners were amazing to me, I was especially impressed with learners who were diagnosed with Asperger

Syndrome (dyslexic with high functioning autism.) and told they would never learn to read; with men and women who had had Strokes, again, without hope they would be able to access their brains in the way they had prior to their brain injury. It goes without saying, my two experiences with two women who had Alzheimer syndrome only opens the door to what is possible with our instruction.

The second was to have Dr. Schwartz observe our students during their transformation! And when he did then the bells-and-whistles went off! He, based on his education and research experience, could make hypothesis about what the brain required to cause a transformation! Dr. Schwartz could say, this behavior changed so therefore we are having an impact on the occipital and broca's part of the brain and possibly other parts of the brain. When you learn to read with our Universal Reading Method you can thank Dr. Barry Schwartz PhD, (neuroscience) for bringing the research findings to it that invited you to do so.

Dr. Schwartz observed one of our adult learners, Lewis, who had two strokes, not only return to reading, but also the subtle changes of the brain that had impacted the slurring of speech and the overall use of the left side of the body for walking. He watched us, in 2 1/2 hours organize neuro-plasticity in Lewis's brain! This observation moved Dr. Schwartz into action, the action I had been waiting for for several years. It was then that I experienced a beam of light that was lighting up our direct path on our road to research at a prominent University!

After his observations of Lewis, Dr. Schwartz was off to talk to one of his MEG research friends, Ming-Xiong Huang, at the

University of California at San Diego about the Universal Reading
Method instruction being studied in a neuroplasticity, brain imaging
experiment!

From the time that Dr. Schwartz first introduced our Universal
Reading Method and its impact on the brain to Dr. Huang took
approximately 5 years for us to be honored by an invitation to be a
part of a study.

The road to Research was not always a direct road. Our
research at UCSD was made possible because the, two-of-twenty in
the nation that is enclosed in a sound proof room, MEG Scanner and
Dr. Ming Huang were brought to UCSD in 2004! Finally, we will be
able to explain, with scientific data, and answer many of the "Why
and How" questions we have had while observing our learners
transform in 2 1/2 hours. We will begin to receive the kind of data
and attention our mind and life-changing process requires to reach our
goals to be received by and teach the world to read, English, we have
planned!

So, in 2014 with an authorization to begin research at UCSD, I
returned to San Diego from, our field research and teaching on Maui,
where I was transforming challenged readers, to begin formatting our
Scientific study, for UCSD. Dr. Schwartz reviewed my success of
transforming learners, with Asperger Syndrome, Dyslexia, PTSD,
ADD, and, Strokes and Alzheimers Syndrome. It was obvious that
we needed to share with the world what we were experiencing in the
field and to establish ourselves with the type of credibility a MEG
Brain Imaging Study would provide.

However, the Universe was not quite ready for us to begin our

Research at UCSD as soon as was expected. Apparently, there was a new Dean who now required that our pilot study be funded with $15,000 and provided by us! So, it was back to the drawing board and our search for the $15,000.

Dr. Schwartz and I met several times with Dr. Ming Huang and he was excited about what we had accomplished and impressed with the observations that Dr. Schwartz and I had made. I was so excited after that meeting that I asked everyone I know for the $15,000. Being an entrepreneur is not a shy path! After soliciting multiple individuals and CEO's of successful education related companies we: Barry Schwartz Phd, myself, and a fine man, the Founder of the John Corcoran Foundation, John Corcoran decided to apply for a Grant with the Farrel Foundation, in Orange County! In August of 2018 we were informed that The John Corcoran Foundation had been awarded the $15,000 funds that were required to fund the Scientific research at UCSD.

After ten years of watering our Bamboo Tree, it was actually beginning to grow in leaps and bounds! We have increased our efforts to transform students at Literacy Foundations, Community Colleges, Magnate Schools, and on our www.universalreadingmethod.com website, with Affiliate Relationships, sharing our 2 1/2 hour course! Currently, anyone who wishes to learn to read English can do so for $297.00. If you wish to become an Affiliate you can sign up for free and we will pay you 1/2 of our charge to each student and provide you your own personal, Universal Reading Method, URL.

We are very exciting to announce that we will begin with our first Research subject at UCSD in the first week of August, 2019.

In the meantime, we have brought on Allison Shreeve, an Internet Marketing Guru and Founder of Integrity Marketing Corp in Australia to design and provide for us our internet marketing strategy.

The study will proceed as follows:

We will sign up five subjects for our research! Each of our subjects will be several years behind in their English Reading Skills. All subjects will receive the WRAT4 pretest to determine their current reading capability and at the end of the instruction the WRAT4 post reading test! All ten will receive an MRI and MEG Brain Scan before and MEG after the instruction. All five of our subjects will watch, and verbally participate, in the 2 1/2-hour Universal Reading Method instruction. The subjects will be drawn from a pool of students found at the local Colleges and living in the San Diego community!

Our goal is to reveal what is happening within the brain when our students receive our video instruction. What parts of the brain are being impacted. What changes in the brain are taking place! Basically, we are observing if and how a process of Neuro-plasticity is taking place in the brain after 2 1/2 hours of the Universal Reading Method instruction.

After all of the data has been collected then a scientific data-evaluator, at UCSD, will analyze and provide us with a clear view of what took place in the brain. We feel that our results will have a profound impact on the teaching of reading immediately after UCSD publishes their finding.

We are in contact with the law firms whom are involved in the Literacy Litigation in Detroit and California so as to keep them informed for the purpose of implementation as a solution to their litigation on behalf of students who are litigating because they did not learn to read during their 12 years of Public School instruction!

When we are able to provide you with the results of our MEG Brain imaging and URM video instruction, we will be adding to this book to keep you informed. It is very exciting for us and something I am confident you will enjoy following as well!

Meanwhile, please, if you have a child, a spouse, a friend or someone you know who is challenged with reading direct them to our website: www.universalreadingmethod.com and/or sign up as an affiliate and receive a 50% commission from us for each person who signs up to learn to read from your personalized and own Universal Reading Method URL.

Thank you for following our journey and all of your support! The Reading Miracle is real and we can change the world!

Capital Partner Opportunity

Universal Reading Method, LLC, a Wyoming Corporation, is pleased to announce we are inviting and available to receive a Capital Business Partner.

The Universal Reading Method has achieved the following:

- Traveled, Researched and Taught our Universal Reading Method across the United States, Canada, across the Pond to the UK, Hawaii in person, on SKYPE to hundreds of challenged learners.
- Online, at www.universalreadingmethod.com with Fusion, a high level conversion program.
- Currently enrolled in a MEG Brain Imaging Study at the University of California at San Diego at the direction of Dr's Ming-xiong Huang and Barry Schwartz (neuroscience) to be completed in 2002.
- Authored our first book, **The Reading Miracle**. A chronicle of a cross-section of challenged learners from around the world who benefited from learning to read English with the Universal Reading Method.
- Partnered with a skilled Internet Marketing Expert, Allison Shreeve (IntegrityMarketingCorporation.com)
- Actively participating with Literacy Organizations, Schools, and Therapist who specialize in reading disorders.

- Building an active group of Affiliate's with a goal of online viral status at www.universalreadingmethod/Affiliate

Please contact Craig Collins at

ureadingmethod@gmail.com or call me, at 858 945 5007

with enthusiasm about joining our team and teaching

the world to read, with our Universal Reading Method.

www.ingramcontent.com/pod-product-compliance
Lightning Source LLC
Chambersburg PA
CBHW031840090426
42741CB00005B/310